OKANAGAN COLLEGE LIBRARY

03692704

GLOBALIZATION &IDENTITY

D1615969

OKANAGAN COLLEGE
LIBRARY
BRITISH COLUMBIA

GLOBALIZATION &IDENTITY

CULTURAL DIVERSITY, RELIGION, AND CITIZENSHIP

PEACE AND POLICY, VOLUME 10

MAJID TEHRANIAN
B. JEANNIE LUM,
EDITORS

TRANSACTION PUBLISHERS
NEW BRUNSWICK (U.S.A.) AND LONDON (U.K.)

LIBRARY

Second Printing 2007

Copyright © 2006 by Toda Institute for Global Peace and Policy Research.
Version of an issue of *Peace & Policy*, Vol. 10, 2006, copyright © 2006 by Toda Institute for Global Peace and Policy Research.

All rights reserved under International and Pan-American Copyright Conventions. No part of this book may be reproduced or transmitted in any form or by any means, electronic or mechanical, including photocopy, recording, or any information storage and retrieval system, without prior permission in writing from the publisher. All inquiries should be addressed to Transaction Publishers, Rutgers—The State University, 35 Berrue Circle, Piscataway, New Jersey 08854-8042.

This book is printed on acid-free paper that meets the American National Standard for Permanence of Paper for Printed Library Materials.

ISBN: 978-1-4128-0561-2
Printed in the United States of America

Contents

Peacenotes

Under the able editorship of Jeannie Lum, this volume of *Peace & Policy* is focusing on globalization and identity. The chapter topics range from theoretical reflections to case studies. They pose the problem, but they also point to possible solutions. All in all, they suggest that in a globalizing world, a layering of identity from local to global is perhaps the most prevalent and appropriate strategy. In such a strategy, the conventional mottos do not make sense. "My country, or my tribe, or my religion, right or wrong" is out of harmony with the realities of a globalizing world. Diasporas have increased physical, social, and psychic mobility. They have often called for hybrid identities. Multiethnic or religious societies, one trillion websites, countless email exchanges, direct satellite television, short-wave radio, and global cellular phones have augmented global communication. To be insular is to be unaware of a world in fermentation.

In the first decade of the twenty-first century, globalization and identity have emerged as the most critical challenges to world peace. State and opposition terrorism are being fought under the dubious aegis of particular identities, religious or secular. Genocides in Yugoslavia, Chechnya, Rwanda, Israel-Palestine, and Sudan have taken place in the name of religion, ethnic cleansing, or competing nationalisms. However, commodity fetishism has proven to be as powerful as identity fetishism. Globalization has whetted consumer appetites. The consuming identities of those exposed to global advertising have sometimes focused on the designer car, the clothing, or the perfume. In response to the rampant consumption of the rich, the poor have often resorted to their cultural identities. Commodity and identity fetishism thus lay out the landscape of a globalizing world.

The articles in this issue promise the dawn of a new global civilization. They may appear as too optimistic. But they have focused on the undercurrents of world system change. On the surface, we are witnessing a dual process of globalization and tribalization. But deeper down, out of the encounter of cultures and civilizations, a new form of consciousness is emerging that understands global interdependence. Government institutions may be lagging far behind such a new consciousness, which is understandable. Governments often defend the status quo. But cultural changes ultimately triumph. The pioneers of a global consciousness are the people who dare to be different.

Majid Tehranian
August 14, 2005

1

Introduction

by B. Jeannie Lum

B. Jeannie Lum is an associate professor of Philosophy of Education in the Department of Educational Foundations, College of Education and a member of the Spark M. Matsunaga Institute for Peace at the University of Hawai'i at Mânoa.

On March 17-20, 2002, the Globalization, Regionalization, and Democratization Planning Conference (GRAD), jointly sponsored by the Toda Institute and the University of Hawai'i Globalization Research Center, was held at Magdalen College, Oxford University. Over the four days, scholars, researchers, and clergymen from all over the world representing eight major regions, engaged in discussion of a range of topics on global problems and divided into working groups that continued for the next three years. Our team included ten final participants from different nations—Australia, Canada, France, Germany, India, Jamaica, Lithuania, Russia, United Kingdom, and the United States.

This volume of *Peace & Policy* addresses the overarching question, "What are the effects of globalization in the areas of culture, ethnic diversity, religion and citizenship in attaining a sense of global identity?" In seeing each of these areas as critical aspects of human identity, it is impossible to speak singly about one without reference to one or more of the others. Human identity evolves as a cultural phenomenon. At the core of individual and collective group identities are philosophical and/or religious beliefs and values that define the perspectives that persons take in understanding their place in society, their relationship to themselves and others in their community, and importantly, their definitions of what con-

stitutes a meaningful life. The problematic for attaining a sense of global identity is in our ability to preserve the richness of human cultural diversity at all levels of local, regional, national, and global communication and exchange.

We saw this as a Janus-faced dilemma whereby globalization could have both negative and positive consequences in its impact on the shaping of human identity. It was important for us also to examine our own group behavior by "walking the talk." Being and acting globally meant not enforcing one particular view as dominant over another and not reducing our task to one common theme, but retaining the complexity and originality of each member's theoretical voice and concerns. Given our different backgrounds, it was important to manage the operations of the group in such a way that all members were *heard*. We talked about the multitude of disciplinary perspectives and approaches in our professions, and in some cases, our dissimilar opinions about what we should produce as a group, what audiences were important to reach, and even the format in which our articles should be written. We hope we have contributed to the literature that looks at this family of concepts in relationship to the problem of global identity and further inspired others to join in this conversation.

We dedicate this volume in remembrance of one of the members of our group, Jerry

Chang, a former vice president of the East-West Center and local coordinator of the Cooperation Circles for Peace for the United Religious Initiative. Chang also founded and served as president of Humanity United Globally, a nonprofit he endowed to promote international youth concerts and information events such as the Waging Peace Conference at the Hawai'i State Capitol in 2002. He founded the World Vision Youth Ambassadors program, which brought fifty youths from fifty different countries together for training and study. Chang was also a member of the Interfaith Open Table, and he started the Hawai'i chapter of Habitat for Humanity in 1988.

In Part I, the authors address broad issues, and reexamine the current globalization of the world in light of the traditions from which human civilizations have evolved. The threat of globalization to homogenize cultures through economic hegemony and political domination finds its strongest resistance in the core belief systems upon which human civilizations have developed and survived. Religious ideals and philosophies of living are deeply embedded and inseparable from human understandings of private and public identity. Beliefs and values guide persons in their actions and in the ways they interpret their lives as meaningful in everyday living, but also they define our collective identity in the establishment of our social, cultural, and political public institutions. Moreover, two conditions of our modern world have great influence on globalization today— the limitations of our shared natural resources, and the capacity of modern technologies to reach beyond national boundaries to sustain, destroy, or create life. Groff, Camilleri, and Mofid carve out a broad framework from which we can begin thinking about a global identity and how our identity is represented in the ways civiliza-

tions have emerged and developed. We need to place this problem in the context of our philosophical, religious, and cultural history to ensure the survival of our civilization(s) and the recreation of a sense of our humanity.

Linda Groff opens this section by introducing us to one of the major conversations of our times. In *The Dialogue or Clash of Civilizations*, she focuses our attention on Samuel R. Huntington's thesis—that the Cold War would be followed by a clash of civilizations—and whether or not a more desirable outcome, such as a "dialogue of civilizations" is possible. After describing various other ideas about civilizations and other authors' responses to Huntington, Groff provides her own perspective centered on our need to *reframe our worldviews* in ways that include acknowledgement of both diversity and interdependence between the world's peoples. Groff details how such a shift in consciousness and identity might look, and lists some policy recommendations that may be useful for decision-makers at local, state, and regional levels seeking to further these ends.

Joseph A. Camilleri proposes that *citizenship* is a "central ordering concept in the organization of human affairs" of Western cultures, but one that is fraught with problems if a notion of global citizenship is to become a reality in theory and practice. In *Citizenship in a Globalizing World*, Camilleri traces the history of the concept of citizenship and identifies the subtle transformations of the notion through Greek, Roman, Medieval Christendom, the Enlightenment, and modern times. Where earlier understandings of what it meant to be a citizen of a city, state, or nation were tied to an active, participatory, communitarian ethic of shared values and intersubjective discourse, in modern times, this has been replaced by a concept of private, passive, individual rights and preferences, safe-guarded by an elected "representative" elite in exchange for membership benefits of national organization. The Enlightenment project of democratic citizenship has failed and the image of the universal man endowed with inalienable human rights to make his own history has become that of the alien-ated man, driven by interests of the market economy, devoid of social commitment and responsibility for a common good.

Globalization is a fragmenting process in rapid development, movement, and ex-changes of people, goods, money, and in-formation. Camilleri suggests that the complex dynamic and mosaic of postmodern cultural and political life must seek a new sense of global identity that goes beyond the state-centric form of citizenship embedded in Western traditions. As an al-ternative, he turns to eastern religions and cultures (Hinduism, Buddhism, Confucian-ism, and Islam) to show how a communal ethic integrated with respectfulness for hu-man dignity underlies many of these tradi-tions and is infused with expectations of benevolent forms of governance. He goes beneath the commonplace political rheto-ric that misrepresents the organizational ethos of Eastern countries and explains how Western ideals of citizenship may be inter-preted according to Eastern religious and philosophical beliefs and values, as well as how Eastern sensibilities of human "rights" are richly interwoven aspects of personal, social, and political cultural identities.

Camilleri believes that continuing efforts for dialogues across cultural and religious boundaries in today's inter-religious and in-terfaith organizations can become a force for healing, and even nurture a *radical* ethic in the evolving organization of human affairs.

Kamran Mofid argues in his chapter, *Globalization for the Common Good,* that the marketplace as the primary engine of globalization is not just an economic sphere, but also a "region of the human spirit." He believes that the globalized world economy, particularly in the most recent decades, has had disastrous affects on our socioeco-nomic, political, cultural, and environmen-tal life. Mofid proposes that traditional economic imperatives have lost sight of the aim to widen the base of prosperity for the many instead of the few. He defines "glo-balization for the common good" as an economy of sharing, and of global values—such as altruism, inclusion, universality, fraternity, sympathy, empathy, sharing, se-curity, envisioning, enabling, empowering, solidarity, etc., and believes that economic and business interests must embrace the spiritual assets of the community.

Majid Tehranian raises the problem of identity in a globalizing world in "Rethink-ing Civilization." In addition to local, na-tional, and regional identities, he advocates the assumption of global identity, respon-sibility, and citizenship.

In Part II, we move further into the com-plex issues of diversity in religions, belief systems, and the sources and social proclivi-ties for communitarian commitments, val-ues, and ethics previously laid forth. This set of papers looks at some of the common ways in which we think of our world as divided, both geographically and region-ally, according to cultural, ethnic, and reli-gious identities. They suggest theoretical and practical ways in which we can think and act to overcome our dualistic frame-works and to recreate new sensibilities that honor, accept, and reinterpret differences in our capacity for creativity and symbolic language. Leeds, Korobov, and Gupt show how this reconceptualization process has already begun and how new spaces continue to be opened up in scholarship and among the public to take action guided by global awareness.

INTRODUCTION

Christopher A. Leeds explores the religious and philosophical belief systems traditionally seen as separating the Eastern part of the world from the West. He shows how there are common overlapping ideals and values that cross boundaries in today's ecological and sustainability movements initiated by environmentalists, eco-feminists, animal rights advocates, and spiritually based groups about global warming, the careless destruction of our natural resources, and the permissive policies of governments. In *Eco-Theology, Environmentalism and Process*, Leeds approaches the problem of globalization by looking at its impact on the environment and the role religion plays in providing an "anthroposcopic" worldview that is nature-centered and facilitates ecological sustainability in which humans form part of the cosmic order. Leeds contrasts this with the current "anthropocentric" worldview that sees humans as dominating, controlling, and manipulating the natural world. He asserts that there are complementary values between Eastern religions—Buddhism, Taoism, Confucianism, and Western views of some classical Christian theologians that facilitate the coming together of cultures towards a greater understanding on how to handle the present ecological plight of our world. Leeds elaborates on two approaches to the environment—*shallow* and *deep* ecology—and their roots in Process Theology and Eco-Theological views. Shallow ecology considers human interests and the management of environmental problems within existing limitations of Western instrumental worldviews that promote gradual modifications in technology, behavior, and public policy. The latter goes to the heart of the matter by questioning our worldview assumptions and presuppositions about our humanity and our human identity in its relationship to nature.

Vladimir Korobov, in *Models of Global Culture*, looks at the impact of globalization on cultures and human identity. He provides an analysis of globalization as primarily an economic and technological process that, when intensified, may have contrary effects that stimulate reactions among cultural groups who are seeking to retain and rediscover their particularity, localism, and difference in their individual, national, and/or collective identities.

The paradox of existing trends in market globalization is, on the one hand, "the elimination of the universalism of the human being in the name of another" and secondly, "a country's ability to build itself depends upon having its own distinct cultural character." Korobov characterizes the mechanisms of nationalizing and hybrid cultures as falling short or succeeding as models for a *global culture*. He proposes a third alternative: "My point is that global culture is not any particular model of culture (American, Chinese or Russian); it is an art of interpretation and to participate in global culture means to be able to understand artifacts of other cultures in their own contexts, and to produce (by means of art, literature or science) new knowledge codes for understanding reality and the self." Thus, two main functions of global culture are the decoding, interpretation, and reconstruction of local symbols, and the creation of new universal symbols by means of artistic and creative activities. Korobov's creative wisdom thesis submits that the ability for persons to sustain the historical legacy of their own traditions by deepening the process of understanding and regeneration through symbolic means, while at the same time continuing an open communication and interaction with other cultures to create new knowledge, will contribute to the building of a global culture that transcends, yet accounts for local and national identity.

Bharat Gupt discusses the problems with contemporary definitions of pluralism that have been reduced from thousands of years of metaphysical, religious, and ethical debates to mean merely the "tolerance of diverse faiths and cultural habits." He criticizes the superficial ways in which "small matters of ethnic distinctions' such as food habits, dress codes, manners and customs, obscure the deeper more significant issues of religious diversity. Gupt advances his perspective to include the institution of schooling and how, in India, under the British system, religious and moral education was kept out of formal education under the authority of the secular state. The divisions between Muslim and Hindu faiths run deep, and Gupt suggests that the fear of religious instruction presumes that knowing about the faith of others is detrimental to the security and freedom of a child's beliefs, and is ultimately counterproductive to pluralistic goals because it breeds intolerance.

Gupt argues that if plurality is to succeed, it must be promoted in a new public space where religious dialogue is possible. Gupt describes how religious plurality can become integrated into the school curriculum. From his experience in developing policymaking exercises in religious education in India, he sees that religious texts and ideas are most effective when they are taken as part of the expression of the cultural arts and scientific heritage of a country, such as in music, dance, poetry, painting, drama, mythology, and traditional medicine. Gupt provides several recommendations for the transformation of India's school system in teaching the Heritage Curriculum as Heritage Activity that incorporates many of the activity-based modes of

instruction we associate with progressive education.

Part III delves further into the multiple dimensions of the globalizing effects of economic expansion and political strife as experienced by different cultures at local and regional levels. Religion, ethnicity, and nationalism become interwoven in the collective identities of small communities. Both positive and negative consequences result in the introduction of new products, new societal problems, and newly acquired social roles that require new and changing modes of adaptation in order for people to continue to live together harmoniously. Ogunrinade and Riggs provide examples where globalization is a means of breaking down particular and localized identities of different religious and ethnic groups that may either fragment the social fabric of a culture or unify it by spurring increased growth and development. Political leadership plays a critical role in the ultimate outcome of our current crisis by how it conceptualizes and manages the problems of globalization in policy decision-making.

Audrey E. Kitigawa, in *Globalization as the Fuel of Religious and Ethnic Conflicts*, explains how the development of global financial markets and transnational corporations has increased steadily in their domination over national and global economies in the past twenty-five to fifty years. She details how this has enabled the disproportionate distribution of wealth into the hands of the few, and the resulting internal strife among resource-rich developing countries. Africa, in particular, is the scene of many violent conflicts that are presented as cultural conflicts caused by religious and ethnic divisions. But in reality, it is groups competing over natural resources—government, tribal warlords, rebels, and others who control the wealth—that cause havoc among their people.

INTRODUCTION

Kitigawa takes Nigeria as an example of political manipulation of religious and ethnic groups to divert attention away from the real problems of social and economic marginalization and degradation of the people. Economic globalization as it exists in its current state is in need of major reform. Kitigawa insists, "There must be greater transparency on the inner workings of international financial institutions, and changes to their organizational structures of governance and accountability, as well as to their policies and practices." An open door to the process of decision-making where financial or commercial interests are involved, improvements in banking conditions, oversight of the loaning practices of international financial institutions that prevent corruption and squander, government responsibility for implementing transparency and accountability that stems from corruption and abuse, and the continued work towards peace and the alleviation of human suffering are needed to combat the negative consequences of globalization.

Adelani F. Ogunrinade looks at the impact of globalization on the socio-political transformations of multiethnic societies, using Nigeria as a case study. In *Turmoil in Babel*, Ogunrinade cites the positive and negative consequences of globalization due to the unevenness of the distribution of wealth among various sectors of Africa's economy. From a social transformational analytical framework, Ogunrinade posits that in the absence of a moderated political economy, globalization has greater social consequences because new forms of social and cultural destabilization erupt, and undermine the ability of a nation to control its economic destiny.

Ogunrinade traces the failure of political and military leadership in Nigeria in the transition of an agricultural-based economy to one dependent on oil, and the ensuing

corruption that eventually led to state bankruptcy. Ogunrinade identifies one of the paradoxes of advanced globalization as its reversion to rising forms of particularization and ethnic religious cleavages between tribal groups, localism at the expense of globalization, and a rebirth of ethnic irredentism, regionalism, and factionalism. Other problems such as shifts in the labor migration patterns of Nigerian professionals, electronic credit card scams, and drug trafficking are other consequences of globalization. He describes how the pubic media contributed in flaming the fire of ethnic and religious tensions.

What is the solution to Nigeria's future? Ogunrinade sees that the simple mantra of reduction in corruption, more peace and conflict resolution, responsive governance, higher investments in human capital, or increased food supply—often do not take into account the history of Nigeria or Africa's past problems. Two movements that appear unique and potentially beneficial are the "federal character principle" among Nigeria's elite to manage ethnic plurality and power sharing among a mix of geographical zones and religious/ethnic pluralistic lines with a rotational presidency. In addition, increased globalization has drawn the attraction of world opinion on issues such as human rights, gender rights, and governance, subjecting Nigeria and many African countries to the new norms of international law, which put into place policies and practices against local corruption.

Fred W. Riggs, in *Globalization and Religion on the Web*, looks at how the Worldwide Web has become an effective medium in the globalization of religious movements and a resource for the furthering of doctrines by religious communities. He characterizes different religious groups and outlines the purposes for which religious communities utilize web sites to propagate their own views. Riggs' article is a good example of how religious diversity is a direct outcome of the technology of globalization and how religious groups take advantage of this medium to achieve their aims. However, it leaves open a question about disposition displayed across a wide variety of cultural expressions often seen as antithetical to the *spiritually based* motives of religious missions. Parenthetically, this question raises the problem of globalizing influences on human identity, its cultural coherence, and authenticity.

The Dialogue or Clash of Civilizations

by Linda Groff

Linda Groff is a professor of political science & future studies at California State University, Dominquez Hills, and Director, Global Option Consulting.

Dialogue versus Clash of Civilizations

Globalization, with its many meanings, has generated a great deal of controversy and debate about its impact on different groups of people. Theses like Huntington's (1993, 1996) "clash of civilizations" predict the replacement of the Cold War conflict with conflicts between civilizations in the twenty-first century, but there are other more positive ways in which civilizations may interact in the global environment. In this chapter, the effects of globalization, as well as localization, are examined through the framework of civilizations. Increasing interactions among diverse peoples help create an increasingly interdependent world, which requires reframing of how different civilizations relate to each other (i.e., via dialogue instead of clash).In reconceptualizing this debate, attention to a whole systems worldview that honors *both* the unity *and* the diversity of the world's peoples, cultures, and civilizations would be of great value.

Definitions of Terms

In recent years, there has been an increasing interest in civilizations, or groupings of cultures with similar underlying values and lifestyles, and their past and future evolution. Inter-ethnic conflict within countries has increased since the end of the Cold War, and terrorist conflicts have emerged, involving state, transnational, and non-state actors. Since September 11, 2001, terrorism has dominated world politics, despite the fact that terrorism has been around much longer. Huntington (1993, 1996) focuses much attention on the evolution of conflict, maintaining that the major conflicts in future global politics will be driven by culture, rather than by economy or ideology, and clashes between different civilizations will dominate. A more desirable outcome would be a dialogue of civilizations, but for such a dialogue to occur, a host of positive tools, such as those provided by the fields of intercultural communication and inter-religious dialogue, as well as conflict resolution and negotiation skills, and a commitment to various forms of peace building and nonviolence, will be necessary.

There have been various attempts to define and classify civilizations into different types (Chandler, 1992; Huntington, 1993, 1996; Toynbee and Caplan 1972), and classical macrohistory studies of civilizations have been done in the past (Galtung and Inayatullah 1997). Huntington (1993) characterizes civilization as the largest cultural grouping with which people identify short of humanity as a whole. Civilization can include whole groupings of cultures with similar underlying values and lifestyles. Examples include European, East Asian, South Asian, Arab/Islamic, Slavic, African, and Latin civilizations.

Culture is what gives meaning to life; it is learned, shared, patterned behavior as reflected in technology, tools, social organizations, values, and ideas.

Civilizations began with the rise of ancient empires, following preliterate, pre-civilizational societies; and will be followed by a post-civilizational world in the twenty first century, now that all civilizations are interacting with each other and realizing that their culture or civilization is only one version of "reality"; not the only one (Chandler 1992). Macrohistory examines history's evolution by focusing on broad changes in civilization over broad periods.

Views of Civilizations

Events of September 11, 2001, and other terrorist events, underscore Huntington's warning of a "clash of civilizations" replacing the old Cold War conflict, in this case Muslim versus Western civilizations. Huntington's views have been controversial and have generated a true global debate on the issue. But there is a range of different views on the future of civilizations, and how globalization will affect that future.

One common anthropological view mourns the damage to, and destruction of, non-Western cultures by Western cultures. There is a fear that global cultural homogenization based on the predominance of Western values and lifestyles is threatening the survival of other civilizations and cultures worldwide (Maybury-Lewis, 1992). Sometimes related to this view is the notion that non-Western values and cultures are superior to those of the West. An opposite view sees Western culture as the wave

of the future (Cahill, 1995,1998; Van Doren 1991). Another view posits that civilizations need not rise and fall; they can survive if they have enough energy to meet new challenges as these arise (Toynbee 1972).

A view of Western civilization becoming overly materialistic (sensate) in the 1930s led to a prediction then of a future swing in the pendulum towards spiritual (ideational) values or spiritual and material (idealistic) values (Sorokin, 1985). There is a parallel concern today with the increasing materialization of non-Western civilizations, and the hope that they will not totally lose their spiritual roots as they undergo rapid development and modernization. Yet another view sees an emerging global future which honors and dynamically balances Western and non-Western values, cultures, and worldviews within a larger, global, whole systems context (Smoker and Groff, 1996). This draws upon traditional Taoist worldviews on the dynamic unity of opposites. And Fons Trompenaars (1998) sees the possibility of a true "reconciliation" in the future between formerly opposing, underlying cultural values—such as Eastern and Western, Japanese and "American" values.

P.R. Sarkar (1987, 1999) characterizes civilization by a cyclical power rotation between four groups in the following order: warriors, intellectuals, entrepreneurs, and workers, with each coming to power because of certain strengths they possess, and later losing power because of particular weaknesses that emerge in their exercise of power. Sarkar's model is based on the Indian caste system, and it is therefore fascinating that the Internet (a Western invention) has evolved through the first three stages of Sarkar's model, with the fourth stage predictably emerging next. Another view of traditional civilizations as representing different learned maps or versions of reality (not the territory or ultimate reality), finds these versions to be available as mindsets to be donned when appropriate, for in an interdependent world there can be no fixed worldviews containing all truth (Chandler, 1992).

Stage views of civilizations are also represented in the literature, such as those that see advances in technology driving civilizations through universal stages – agricultural, industrial, and information age stages (Toffler, 1980). Tehranian (2002) sees hunting and gathering, agricultural, commercial/trading, industrial, and informatics ages as examples.

Other "futures" of civilizations see movement towards spiritual values increasingly replacing material values, leading to the eventual creation of the "Noosphere"— a sphere around the earth that would link all the minds of humanity together (Teilhard de Chardin, 1965). These views presaged the emergence of the Internet as the infrastructure for an emerging global brain or mind of humanity. Barbara Marx Hubbard (1993) sees the future going beyond traditional cultures, civilizations, and religions to create something totally new, that is, a great evolutionary leap leading to the emergence of a "universal human" connected to universal spiritual values, going out to explore the universe. Finally, a view common in science fiction sees an evolution to space-age civilizations beyond earth, with the possibility of encounters with extraterrestrial life, and an even greater diversity of civilizations, races, and species. Who can forget *Star Trek,* and its claims to "go where no man/person has gone before," and to honor the "prime directive" and its notion of non-intervention in the evolution of other species' civilizations? *Star Trek* created a culture of dealing with great diversity from a positive, constructive perspective, and it undoubtedly contributed

to the enduring popularity of the series (Friedman, 1999).

What is essential is that a "dialogue of civilizations"—including a dialogue of religions as an important component of civilizations—increasingly replace Huntington's "clash of civilizations." A number of organizations are involved in facilitating the dialogue of religions, including the Council for a Parliament of the World's Religions and the United Religions Initiative, among many others. A number of significant books have also documented the importance of this dialogue of civilizations and religions (Beversluis, 2000; Mische and Merkling, 2001; Tehranian and Chappell, 2002; Tehranian, forthcoming). These books document what world news often does not, namely that peoples of diverse cultures, civilizations, and religions from around the world are all reaching out to each other in important ways, and are using dialogue to create better understanding and respect. These efforts represent important alternatives to Huntington's "clash of civilizations," and the future of the world depends on these alternatives being realized.

Further Reflections

Culture has superficial aspects (dress, greetings, food, etc.) that can change more quickly, and deeper levels, where change occurs much more slowly. The United States has been known as a "melting pot" of cultures, but now the "salad bowl" image of unity amidst great diversity is seen as a more appropriate metaphor. Likewise, the fear of Western cultural imperialism creating a homogenized global culture (one scenario for the future) may be occurring on a superficial level, but perhaps not as much at deeper levels where culture changes much more slowly. This suggests that, while aspects of a global culture are being created on one level, on deeper levels people will continue to value their own diverse cultures in their everyday lives. As people move more quickly into the future, they may also return more to their own roots to hold on to what is really important and meaningful to them from their respective cultures. In these various ways, people will both stay connected to their past as well as ensure their movement into the future.

In an interdependent world, it is vitally important that everyone realizes that cultures are all different, socially learned maps of reality, but they are not ultimate reality, nor are cultures fixed or static or immune from outside influence. Cultures and civilizations can conquer other cultures and on the surface predominate, but sometimes the values and behaviors of the conquered culture survive in various mutated ways, or even eventually co-opt the conquering culture. Possible examples might eventually include Native Americans in the dominant U.S. culture; indigenous peoples in Australia or New Zealand; and Tibetans in China. When the conquered culture or civilization has values needed by, but lacking in, the dominant culture, this can happen. Since more material cultures often conquer less material, but often more spiritual cultures, it is these very spiritual values (of holism and interdependence with all of life) that the dominant culture lacks, but needs to rebalance itself, especially when its technology becomes so advanced and potentially destructive. This is the stage at which humans are on earth today. Unfortunately, much cultural damage can be done before this rebalancing occurs, however. Without a reframing of worldviews to acknowledge diversity and interdependence among the world's peoples, dangers of conflicts and wars among civilizations, cultures, and re-

ligions remain very real (Galtung, 1990; Huntington, 1993).

All cultures and civilizations must adapt to global interdependence today and reframe how they relate to other cultures and civilizations. Fundamentalist views—holding that one's own civilization, culture, nation, or religion is the only valid one—become increasingly dysfunctional in an interdependent world that requires respect among cultures and an ability to work together. Black and white thinking—whether of Bin Laden's Islamic fundamentalism and attack, or of the Bush administration's decision to invade Iraq without an international consensus—has greatly increased the polarization of the world. It has fueled support for Huntington's thesis of a "clash of civilizations." Such policies are out of touch with what is needed for an interdependent world.

An alternative hypothesis for the future is that as people from different cultures increasingly interact with each other, communities and individuals can each form unique syntheses of all the different cultural influences that have impacted their lives. In short, people's "identity" will increasingly cross boundaries between different cultures and civilizations. Much intercultural creativity can be unleashed from such interactions within societies and within individuals, who must seek ways within themselves to make sense of and reconcile these diverse cultural influences in their lives. While this process is not always easy, it is a process that all humanity is going through today in varying degrees.

The best framework is to view all cultures and civilizations as having something important to contribute to the world, based on those strengths that each has developed from their own unique histories, experiences and environmental requirements, with no culture or civilization having all the answers. In the future (as in the past), people can enrich their own lives by being open to learning from other cultures, while continuing to value what is important from their own cultural roots. One can thus look at each culture or civilization as bringing different gifts to the table of humanity today. This framework can only work, however, if people can be open to learning from, and respecting, cultural diversity.

Two hypothetical, archetypal, opposite cultural worldviews are possible, with most cultures falling somewhere in between these extremes, though often more towards one pole than the other: (1) a homogenized, whole systems worldview (especially characteristic of non-Western civilizations); and (2) a segmented worldview—where everything is separate from each other (especially characteristic of nineteenth-century Western worldviews). A homogenized, whole systems worldview sees everything as part of an interconnected, larger whole, including collective identity, humanity being a part of nature, spirit immanent in everything, and energy connecting everything, as acupuncture sees the human body. A segmented worldview sees reality divided into separate parts, including individual identity, being separate from nature, God as separate and "on high," and reality divided into separate parts in the Western scientific method.

The seeking of common ground between the world's diverse cultures and civilizations illustrates the possibility of a third, alternative, complex whole systems worldview emerging today—of unity amidst great diversity. For example, people may be seeking ways to have individual and group identities, as well as global, national, and local identities; to honor both spiritual and material values; to be open to both Eastern and Western cultures, as well as indigenous cultures; and to honor both tra-

dition and development or modernization. We are increasingly living in a both/and world, not an either/or world. This emerging worldview can perhaps be characterized by one or more of the following elements: seeing "reality" as a dynamic "dance of life" between opposites (Taoist view); as a "reconciliation" between opposites (Trompenaars and Hampton-Turner 1998b); or at least being able to use aspects of different cultures and civilizations as appropriate (Chandler, 1992), and realizing that all cultures have different gifts to contribute to humanity today that can collectively benefit us all.

The future of cultures and civilizations is a complex, multifaceted topic that makes today's world both an exciting and challenging one in which to live. Complex issues of cultural identity will continue to dominate the world, as people seek ways to preserve their traditional local cultural values amidst increasing intercultural interactions and globalization. It is clear that preserving cultures in their pure form (if indeed this ever existed, which is doubtful) will become increasingly difficult in the future, especially with a global economy, but with global telecommunications as the emerging global brain of humanity, the diversity of humanity can hopefully continue to be represented.

Policy Proposals

Despite all the polarizing effects of terrorism and the Iraqi war, and concerns of people about globalization's failure to deal adequately with social, employment, and environmental concerns, the world's peoples must still seek ways to inhabit this planet together in a way that increasingly benefits all. The challenges are enormous, but so are the opportunities. Whether the transition to a healthier, interdependent global community is more tumultuous or not depends on various factors, but one way or another such a transition is occurring. Policies that can help smooth the transition include the following:

- Incorporate curriculum on global issues and other countries and cultures, civilizations, and religions into the education of all students starting at an early age and continuing through university education. This education should also include interacting with peoples of diverse backgrounds in one's own community.
- Promote interactive centers and museums honoring the cultural and religious diversity of their inhabitants by cities and communities around the world.
- Increase cultural exchange programs for students abroad, and opportunities for people to work in other cultures through their jobs. While working abroad, take time to really learn about and interact with people from that other culture.
- Increase education in intercultural communication, interreligious and intercivilizational dialogue, and build conflict resolution and nonviolence skills, to give people positive tools for dealing with cultural, civilizational, and religious diversity.
- Elect leaders in countries that honor our global interdependence and the need to work with other countries to provide global, not just national, leadership on pressing global issues, including working through the United Nations.
- Encourage media around the world to write about and broadcast stories of positive intercultural, interreligious,

and intercivilizational peace building efforts, not only violence to defend cultures, religions, and civilizations. The media's tendency to focus largely on current crises, conflict, and violence gives people around the world a distorted view of what is already happening that is positive, and people need positive examples to emulate if they are also to change.

It is also vital that the more developed parts of the world reach out to the less developed peoples of the world, so that all can increasingly participate in, and contribute to, this emerging, culturally complex, global community. If this does not happen, then it is clear that more violent, conflict-laden scenarios will dominate the future. Globalization must be seen to benefit all peoples, not only the few. The increasing gap between rich and poor, both within and between countries in recent years, and the continuing poverty that exists in many parts of the world, must somehow be reversed, and greater educational opportunities must become available to people globally. Without these commitments, no amount of intercultural communication or interreligious/intercivilizational dialogue will be able, on its own, to create more desirable scenarios, rather than a clash of civilizations, for our future.

References

Beversluis, Joel. 2000. *Sourcebook of the world's religions: an interfaith guide to religion and spirituality.* Novato, CA: New World Library.

Cahill, Thomas. 1998. *The gifts of the Jews: how a tribe of desert nomads changed the way everyone thinks and feels (Hinges of History, Vol. 2).* New York: Anchor Books and Doubleday.

Cahill, Thomas. 1995. *How the Irish saved civilization (Hinges of History)*. New York: Doubleday.

Chandler, Keith. 1992. *Beyond civilization: the world's four great streams of civilization: their Achievements, their differences and their future*. [S.I.]: Rivendell Publishing Co.

Friedman, Michael J. 1999. *Star Trek: new worlds, new civilizations*. New York: Simon & Schuster.

Galtung, Johan. 1990. Cultural violence. *Journal of Peace Research* (27) 3: 291-305.

Galtung, Johan, and Inayatullah, Sohail, Eds. 1997. *Macrohistory and macrohistorians: perspectives on individual, social, and civilizational Change*. Westport, CT: Praeger.

Hubbard, Barbara Marx. 1993. *The evolutionary journey: a personal guide to a positive future*. San Francisco: Evolutionary Press.

Huntington, Samuel P. 1993. The clash of civilizations. *Foreign Affairs* (72) 3: 22-49.

Huntington, Samuel P. 1996. *The clash of civilizations and the remaking of world order*. New York: Simon & Schuster.

Ikeda, Daisaku, and Tehranian, Majid. 2003. *Global civilization: a Buddhist-Islamic dialogue*. London: British Academic Press.

Maybury-Lewis, David. 1992. *Millennium: tribal wisdom and the modern world*. Alexandria, VA: Distributed by PBS Video.

Mische, Patricia M., & Merkling, Melissa, Eds. 2001. *Toward a global civilization? The contribution of religions*. New York: Peter Lang.

Sarkar, P. R. 1999. *Human society*. Calcutta: Ananda Marga.

Sarkar, P. R. 1987. *Neo-humanism in a nutshell*. Calcutta: Ananda Marga.

Smoker, Paul, & Groff, Linda, 1996. Spirituality, religion, culture, and peace: exploring the foundations for inner-outer peace in the 21st century. *International Journal of Peace Studies* 1 (1): 57-113.

Sorokin, Pitirim. 1985. *Social and cultural dynamics: a study of change in major systems of art, truth, ethics, law, and social relations*. New Brunswick, N. J.: Transaction Publishers.

Tehranian, Majid, & Chappell, David W., Eds. 2002. *Dialogue of civilizations: a new peace agenda for a new millennium*. New York: I.B. Tauris Publishers in association with The Toda Institute for Global Peace and Policy Research.

Tehranian, Majid. (Forthcoming) *Rethinking civilization: communication and terror in the global village*.

Teilhard de Chardin, Pierre. 1965. *The phenomenon of man*. New York: Harper & Row.

Toffler, Alvin. 1980. *The third wave*. New York: Bantam Books.

Toynbee, Arnold, & Caplan, Jane. 1972. *A study of history*. New York: Weathervane Books.

Trompenaars, Fons. 1998. Keynote Address, 24th International Congress of the Society for Intercultural Education, Training, and Research. Tokyo, Japan.

Trompenaars, Fons, & Hampton-Turner, Charles. 1998b. *riding the waves of culture: understanding diversity in global business*. New York: McGraw-Hill.

Van Doren, Charles. 1991. *A history of knowledge: past, present, and future*. New York: Ballantine Books.

Citizenship in a Globalizing World

by *Joseph A. Camilleri*

Joseph A. Camilleri is a Professor of International Relations at La Trobe University, Melbourne. He is a Fellow of the Academy of the Social Sciences in Australia.

Citizenship is hardly a new idea. The meaning we attribute to it today still carries the imprint of the diverse moral and intellectual influences that have shaped the Western tradition. From its philosophical and practical origins in the Greek city-state to the legal norms developed by Republican and later Imperial Rome, the ethical impulses of the Judeo-Christian worldview, and the secularist leanings of the Enlightenment, citizenship has served as a central ordering concept in the organization of human affairs.

Legitimate doubts have nevertheless surfaced as to its current and future relevance. Several questions readily come to mind: Can an idea rooted in the history of the territorially bound state, be it the city-state, the imperial state, the feudal state or the nation-state, still have relevance in the era of globalization? Can the ethos of citizenship respond to the multiple crises of contemporary life? Is it possible or even desirable to breathe new life into a concept that many identify with the particularist identities and allegiances of a bygone age?

This paper argues that both the theory and practice of citizenship are in need of substantial rethinking if they are to meet the challenges of the contemporary human predicament. Such a project is, of course, fraught with difficulty. To have any chance of success, it needs to tap into the extraordinarily rich resource that is the world's civilizational inheritance. As we shall see, the key to this journey—acquiring a clearer sense of the destination and of the signposts along the way—lies in enhancing the dialogical dynamic between different parts of that inheritance. Put simply, citizenship as both idea and practice must be recast in ways that draw sustenance from the dialogue of civilizations.

The Evolution of Citizenship

Though "citizen" derives from the Latin word *civitas*, the idea itself has a much older history, which we can trace back to Hellenic civilization. More specifically, we associate citizenship with the emergence of the Greek *polis* and the development of the twin notions of freedom and equality, which, though barely discernible in Homer's writings, became fully visible in Solon's Athens in the sixth century BC (Beiner 1995: 4-6). Athenian citizenship was in practice reserved for the few, but the privilege and status that it implied rested on a profound understanding of the relationship between politics and humanity, between the public and the private. To be truly human, life had to be lived inside the *polis*. Citizenship meant participation in the life of the community and in the decisions that vitally affected its future. In this important sense the private and private spheres became inextricably intertwined.

While it inherited the Greek legacy of citizenship, Rome substantially modified it. Civic virtue remained a distinguishing characteristic but the participatory ethos was replaced by the rule of law. Both Greek and Roman conceptions of citizenship survived the decline of the Roman Empire, but medieval Christendom shifted the understanding of the person "into the domain of religion and metaphysics." in part by establishing a division between the temporal and the supernatural, between "an earthly city that glorified itself, and a heavenly city that glorified god" (Clarke 1994:11).

The corollary of this shift, implicit in Augustine's doctrine of the two cities (Dods 1871–76: 326–328), was that the profane should be ultimately subordinate to the sacred. In time, the shift was made explicit with the concerted efforts of the church to make secular power subservient to papal power. Paradoxically, at the very time that the Catholic Church seemed at the zenith of its power, its most influential theologian, Thomas Aquinas, countenanced a different path to humane governance. He argued that human law can be perverted if the intention of the lawgiver is not fixed on true good, understood as "the common good regulated according to divine justice." In that event, the tyrannical law is not consistent with reason, and therefore not worthy of obedience by the citizen. The lawgiver may be resisted by dint not of papal edict but of human reason.

Embryonically at least, Aquinas had foreshadowed the decisive shift to human reason as the governing principle in the ordering of human affairs, which several centuries later the Enlightenment would take to its ultimate and secular conclusion. Citizenship became a central plank of the project of modernity (Turner 1994: 155).

The Enlightenment Project

There is no denying that the twin impulses of democracy and nationalism in the late eighteenth century gave rise to a new conception of citizenship of considerable emancipatory potential. A new sense of belonging emerged, which, though simultaneously inclusive and exclusive, gave rise to an understanding of the citizen as "universal man," a species being endowed with inalienable "human" rights, destined to make his own history rather than be made by it.

However, when viewed in all its theoretical and practical complexity, the Enlightenment idea becomes far more ambiguous. Authoritarian power exercised from above was to be transformed into "self-legislated" power arising from the general will (Rousseau) or the "concurring and unified will" of the citizenry (Kant). The democratic impulse that made participation in the community the defining quality of citizenship was not, however, either universally understood or practiced. Maximalist interpretations of democratic citizenship were consistently questioned and often thwarted by minimalist conceptions. In this latter view, the individual remained external to the state, "contributing only in a certain manner to its reproduction in return for the benefits of organizational membership" (Habermas 1995: 261). The participatory, communitarian ethic of shared values and inter-subjective discourse was replaced by a concept of "private" or "passive" citizenship, in which the affairs of government are safely left to a periodically elected elite, citizens concentrate on their individual rights and preferences, and institutions perform a largely instrumental function (Taylor 1989: 178). Though the Western conception of rights has its origins in the Judeo-Christian notion that all men are equal in the sight of God, its modern expression is inextricably linked to the growth of capitalism and to the rise of the merchant and manufacturing classes that gradually displaced the power of monarchs and feudal lords. Over time, it became an integral part of the culture of modernity with its emphasis on rationality, efficiency, predictability, scientific advance, and productivity. The net effect has been to rupture the traditional attachments to local community and to create instead mobile and atomized populations whose claim to humanity rests primarily on the assertion of individual rights vis-à-vis an impersonal, distant and bureaucratized governmental apparatus.

With each advance of the technological age the attractions of individual choice offered by the consumer society assumed increasing importance. Even when the conception of citizenship was widened to encompass the social and economic as well as political dimensions of public life, the stress remained very much on the rights and choices of the individual. Over time citizenship was extended to a wide range of previously excluded groups, including women, workers, Jews, Catholics, and blacks (Marshall 1965: 78–80). But their inclusion was primarily as individual voters, as claimants of rights in the public domain and consumers of goods and services in the marketplace, in short as members of an atomized society. The function of the state was to guarantee the stability of both domains and so ensure in each case relatively satisfied customers.

This project, which we associate with the development of the welfare state and policies of Keynesian demand management, benefited from the unprecedented rates of economic growth registered in much of the Western world between the late 1940s and early 1970s. However, even during the heyday of capitalist peace and prosperity, several voices could be heard questioning the adequacy of political arrangements which reduced citizenship to the relatively passive enjoyment of material entitlements (MacPherson 1962). To begin with, an entitlement to something did not necessarily mean a capacity to exercise that entitlement. Legal, political, and social rights could not be delivered by mere constitutional or legislative fiat. Such delivery would inevitably depend on appropriate political, social, and economic arrangements. In the political arena, constitutional guarantees had to be buttressed by a plurality of power centers, the open and balanced dissemination of information and opinion, and effective access to the protection of the law, especially for the less affluent social strata. In few societies were these requirements wholly or even largely met.

A significant gap soon emerged between the promise and performance of the state. Several developments have been important contributing factors. The first and most obvious is globalization, a complex and multifaceted phenomenon involving successive waves of technical innovation. With it has come the retooling and reorganization of production, large-scale reshaping of transportation and communication systems, and profound changes to rural and urban life. The result is a highly interconnected system of social and economic relationships, with production, trade, and finance brought increasingly under the unifying logic of the world market. Social change can now be said to be global. It unfolds over global space with key actors exercising global reach, reflects a global architecture of power, and gives rise to global norms and principles (Camilleri 1995: 211). In a world of cars, planes, televisions, telephones, and computers—or, as Agnes Heller describes it, a world of "geographic promiscuity"—

we are simultaneously at home everywhere and nowhere (Heller 1995: 16).

A second and closely related development is the rapid movement of people, goods, technologies, money, ideas, images, and information. A globalizing world is by necessity a fragmenting world—a world of traveling cultures, global refugee flows, mushrooming diasporas, and new forms of religious and ethnic polarization. The erosion of existing boundaries and the creation of new ones suggest a third and crucial trend: the diminishing capacity of most societies to draw together their citizens as one, to endow them with a national identity, or enable them to speak with a single voice. At stake is the very capacity of the state to "govern." As Urry puts it, globalization seems to involve some weakening of the power of the social and a corresponding development of "'post-national'citizenship" (Urry 1999: 265). To put it simply, the state, as both political and legal institution, is being squeezed from above, from below, indeed from all sides. Supranational fusion, subnational fission, and transnational interconnectedness are the three dominant trends that are shaping the social, cultural, economic, and ecological landscape.

The complex dynamic of these interconnected currents is calling into question both the state as exclusive ordering principle in the organization of human affairs, and state-centric citizenship as the exclusive form of cultural identification and political allegiance. It is doubtful, to say the least, whether the idea of citizenship can continue to rest on the theory and practice of the nationally bounded society. Put simply, the contemporary challenge is to rethink citizenship in ways that make it relevant to all levels or tiers of governance: municipal, provincial, national, regional, and global. Citizenship will henceforth have to operate in the context of a complex and still evolv-

ing mosaic of responsibilities—obligations on the one hand, and rights and entitlements on the other. This multi-tiered notion of citizenship will inevitably be a periodic source of confusion and even tension, but there is no reason why the multiple loyalties and forms of belonging that it expresses should not be connected to serve the needs of a globalizing, yet culturally and politically heterogeneous world. Involvement in the affairs of one's municipality could be made to enhance, rather than prejudice participation in the affairs of province, nation, region, or the world. Such a synergistic process, however, will not develop automatically. Much effort will be needed to create a legal and organizational framework that reflects and sustains a new conception of citizenship and a new social consciousness. This will not be a case of replacing one tier of governance or one discourse of citizenship with another, or of some new global ethic displacing local and national loyalties. Rather, the new citizenship will cultivate a new public morality that straddles different political spaces and institutions and incorporates the complex mosaic that is cultural and social life in a "plural world."

The Richness of Our Civilizational Inheritance

It may well be that in this emerging ethic the dominant Western discourse will prove less potent or useful than is often assumed. Partly because of its global economic, political, and military dominance, the West has come to believe in the universality of its culture and to measure progress in the light of its own achievements. Western epistemology, with its bias for analytical thinking, has tended to segment and interpret society in zero-sum or adversarial terms where one of the primary functions of conflict is to identify winners and losers. Galtung has characterized "Western social cosmology" as a complex process of fragmentation and marginalization, which separates one individual from another, material from non-material needs, and the private from the public sphere. Though civil and political freedoms are considered the norm in the public sphere, they can coexist, both normatively and practically, with the widespread incidence of poverty and inequality in the private sphere (Galtung 1990: 313).

To draw attention to these shortcomings is not to ignore the very substantial contribution of the Western citizenship tradition and the associated conception of human rights, but rather to indicate that it does not hold a monopoly on citizenship and rights discourse, and that it may not be sufficiently equipped to handle the needs of a politically and culturally plural world. Vincent rightly reminds us that the West has given expression to "three worlds of democracy": one modeled on civil and political rights (Locke); the second on social and economic rights (Marx); and the third on collective rights (Rousseau) (Vincent 1986: 51–52). While all three tendencies have left their mark, it is fair to say that the Lockean view eventually became ascendant. The same three tendencies are also to be found in different civilizations, but here the mix has often assumed a different and subtler complexion. The contemporary international discourse on governance has, of course, developed largely under Western leadership, which helps to explain the dominance of the liberal democratic tradition. The West shaped much of the post-1945 institutional fabric of international relations, as well as national politics in post-colonial societies. Even in the aftermath of political independence, most Third World countries, though formally participating in international forums and negotiations, could exercise only limited leverage over a process that was still driven largely by Western perceptions and priorities.

The new ethic of citizenship and governance will therefore need to reflect a much broader array of civilizational impulses. The emergence of the major religious and ethical traditions during the "Axial Period" (a term coined by Karl Jaspers to describe a period spanning some six centuries from 800 BC to 200 BC) witnessed a radical cultural transformation. It was as if human consciousness had taken a giant turn on its axis. Out of the essentially tribal or ethnic cultures that had hitherto existed, where religion was oriented primarily to the forces of nature, there arose in some parts of the world, quite independently of one another, a number of thinkers, seers, or prophets (e.g., Socrates, Jesus, Mahavira, Buddha, Confucius, Laotzu, Zarathustra, and much later Muhammad). These sages, by subjecting their own tradition to critical examination, refocused human attention on ethical and metaphysical realities and goals that transcended the boundaries of their tribal cultures. These religious and ethical teachings and endeavors became integral to the development of trans-ethnic cultures that we may loosely refer to as civilizations. They did not obliterate the ethnic cultural soil out of which they had grown, but they superimposed on it a higher set of values.

There is no denying that, for all their differences, Hinduism, Buddhism, Confucianism, Islam and the other leading traditions share with Western liberalism and the Judeo-Christian tradition from which it springs a sense of the dignity of human life, a commitment to human fulfillment, and a concern for standards of "rightness" in human conduct (Muzaffar 1999: 25–31).

Common to all traditions is the notion of humane and legitimate governance; although the criteria used to measure legitimacy may vary considerably from one tradition to another. There is, one may reasonably conclude, sufficient common ground between these religious and ethical worldviews to make possible an on-going conversation about human ethics in general, and political ethics in particular (Friedman 1999: 32–55). This is not to question or obscure the many unique characteristics that distinguish each of the civilizational currents and cultural formations. A few general observations on their respective cosmologies may help to convey something of the intricate patterns of commonality and difference.

The Hindu tradition and the caste system that it sustains and legitimizes are, it would seem, fundamentally at odds with notions of freedom and equality. Duties and privileges are assigned on the basis of status or position as specified by caste, age, and sex. On the other hand, the Hindu tradition has tolerated and even encouraged periodic challenges to the prevailing hierarchical order. The caste system itself represents an intricate set of reciprocal relationships, with each group in theory at least respecting "the rights and dignity of the others" (Thompson 1980; Pollis and Schwab 1980). The notion of right, it is true, remains wedded to the concept of duty or *dharma*, one of the four values, the others being wealth (*artha*), happiness (*kama*) and liberation (moksha). For many in the Hindu tradition, however, dharma is not only an end in itself, but the necessary means for the achievement of the other three values. Dharma represents an ideal of society, including "the righting of injustices, the restoring of balance which men in their ignorance or out of selfish passions had disturbed" (Chatterjee 1983: 19).

Buddhism, which emerged as an alternative faith to Hinduism in the fifth century BC, took one strand in Hindu thought, namely the renunciation of self, to its ultimate conclusion. In opposition to the class or caste system, Gautama Buddha established the community of practitioners as a society of equals. For our purposes, several salient features of Buddhist teaching are worth highlighting. The process of evolution (*karma*) that produces human beings represents a series of successful adaptations, in which each individual is the product of countless generations of personal achievement. Upon this evolutionary foundation is built the edifice of "responsible individualism," namely the notion that every individual must take responsibility for his or her actions, since the consequences of those actions will form an integral part of his or her future experience. The knowledge that evolution can be negative as well as positive provides the incentive in the continuing quest for enlightenment, that is, the cultivation of intelligence or wisdom to the transcendent degree. The accumulation of positive karma is made possible by the "eightfold noble path" which in ascending order consists of right views, right thought, right speech, right action, right livelihood, right effort, right mindfulness, and right contemplation (Danto 1987: 74). There are two important points to note here: first, we are all endowed with the potential for enlightenment and liberation; secondly, the radical transformation (or renunciation) of self "does not mean the loss of personality, individuality, or moral responsibility," but the realization of an egoless but truly human personhood (Unno 1988: 140).

The Confucian ethical code, as expressed in the *Four Books*: *The Analects*, *The Great Learning*, *The Doctrine of the Mean*, and *The Book of Mencius,* has largely shaped the Chinese understanding of social relationships. Its two most important contributions were to affirm the perfectibility and educability of the individual and to extend to the commoner a code which was principally derived from the rules and rituals governing the conduct of nobility in feudal China (Tai 1985: 90). As with the Hindu and Buddhist traditions, though without reference to their supernatural or metaphysical cosmology, the Confucian notion of human dignity is embedded not so much in the abstract, purely rational, calculating, autonomous individual favored by Western liberalism as in the person considered in relationship to other persons. It is the set of complex interpersonal relationships, that is the social context, which confers on personhood its meaning and content, hence the importance of manners, customs, and traditions in defining obligations and inextricably linking personal histories.

Notwithstanding the image of political extremism, which Islamic fundamentalism conjures up in the Western mind, and much of the ill-informed stereotyping prevalent in the Western media, the closely related concepts of rights and duties are an integral part of the Islamic faith. Islamic scriptures, beliefs, and traditions may not entirely accord with the Western secular philosophy of the rights of citizens, but a spate of pronouncements and declarations by religious and political leaders suggest that the connections are both numerous and illuminating. For Islam, human rights are not merely or even primarily the rights of individuals, but the rights of the community. In Islamic democracy, freedom is affirmed as the necessary foundation for the establishment of a stable community, in which people cooperate for the sake of the common good. Conversely, the function of the stable community and of the resultant political system is to utilize resources so as

to satisfy human needs and promote human creativity. The four types of freedom identified by Islam (personal freedom, freedom of expression, freedom of religious beliefs, and freedom of private ownership) form part of an "egalitarian, community-oriented approach to freedom," which distances itself from individualistic liberalism in order to stress participation in cultural creation (Said and Nasser 1980: 75–76).

What this all too brief survey suggests is that differences need not be inimical to normative discourse either within or between the major civilizational traditions. It lends weight to two key contentions of this paper. The first is that the emerging inter-civilizational dialogue may benefit as much from difference as from commonality. The second, in part arising from the first, is that the world's major religious and ethical traditions can, in dialogue with each other, richly contribute to the evolving theory and practice of citizenship in the age of globalization. Though each non-Western tradition has its own distinctive ethos and symbolism, several dimensions may be said to characterize their collective—or to be more precise their dialogical—contribution. First, they provide a richer and more varied conception of political space, by establishing a closer connection between human rights and human needs, notably those of the disadvantaged (hence the emphasis on social and economic rights). Secondly, they offer a more holistic understanding of the human condition by establishing a closer connection between rights and obligations and between the individual and the community (hence the dual emphasis on rights and responsibilities). Thirdly, they help to situate citizenship within a larger social context, opening up new possibilities whereby the individual can think and act not as a disaggregated atom but as a member of several overlapping collectivities (hence the emphasis on the rights of communities and peoples—not only the right to self-determination but the right to a healthy environment, the right to food, the right to security, the right to a share of the common heritage of humanity).

The other two dimensions flow from the preceding three but have an importance of their own. The first involves a rejection of Western hegemony, that is, a rejection of the view that the West enjoys a monopoly on the definition of human needs and human rights. Western liberal formulations (and the idea of progress on which they rest) are not seen as applying universally across time and space. Human rights standards may be universal in scope at a given moment, but how these standards are understood and applied is likely to change over time. This brings us to the last aspect of the non-Western contribution to human rights discourse, namely the emphasis on consensual decision-making. If participation is one of the criteria of legitimate governance of a nation's affairs, then presumably the same criterion applies when the arena shifts from national to international governance, be it regional or global. In other words, an international system of law is more likely to command universal respect to the extent that it proceeds by way of negotiation, involves all parties concerned, and incorporates the insights of their respective traditions.

If citizens of the future are to address the immense challenges of the next several decades, they will have to participate in a dialogue of global proportions—global not simply or even primarily in geographic terms, but global in the sense that it cultivates a "global spirituality." Such a dialogue will have to point to the transcendental, yet natural unity of the human family, indeed of all life. Such unity may converge with, but at times also diverge from, the material

unification of a shrinking, consuming and self-consuming, globalizing yet fragmenting world. This will be a dialogue tailored to a new conception of citizenship that puts an entirely different complexion on unity and difference, and allows them to coexist, illuminate, and reinforce each other. Individual citizens will be exalted, not because they are at the center of the political universe, but because they are engaged in an on-going journey of personal transformation inextricably entwined with and contributing to the transformation of social, political, and economic life. Such citizenship will understand that religious and cultural differences are not necessarily a cause for alarm. If properly understood and placed in context, they can be a source of great enrichment. In many ways the challenge of the new citizen is to practice a dialogue that recognizes and taps into the diversity of our civilizational inheritance. Indeed, one of the valuable spin-offs of such a dialogue is that it forces the participants to hold their respective traditions up to critical examination, to rediscover the fundamental ethical impulse that sustains that tradition and to consider ways of adapting it to the new circumstances of our epoch. Civilizational dialogue works best when it fosters a profound soul-searching both within and between civilizations.

Dialogue across cultural and religious boundaries is not, of course, a new idea. It is now well over a century since the 1893 World's Parliament of Religions, held in Chicago, brought together representatives of Eastern and Western spiritual traditions. Today it is recognized as the occasion that formally launched inter-religious dialogue in the modern period. The Council for a Parliament of the World's Religions (CPWR), which officially dates from 1988, was established as a centennial celebration of the 1893 Parliament. The 1993 Parliament adopted *Towards a Global Ethic: An Initial Declaration,* a powerful statement of the ethical common ground shared by the world's religious and spiritual traditions. The dialogical agenda has since gained considerable momentum with several national and international centers making the dialogical agenda a focal point of research, education, and advocacy. These include the Institute for Interreligious, Intercultural Dialogue, the International Interfaith Centre (Oxford), the Global Dialogue Institute, the International Movement for a Just World (Kuala Lumpur), the International Centre for Dialogue Among Civilizations (Tehran), the Centre for World Dialogue (Nicosia), and the Toda Institute itself. Other important institutional developments have included the establishment of the World Council of Religious Leaders and the World Conference of Religions for Peace. More recently, at the instigation of President Khatami, the UN General Assembly adopted in November 1998 a resolution proclaiming the year 2001 as the United Nations Year of Dialogue among Civilizations. In November 2001, the General Assembly adopted the *Global Agenda for Dialogue among Civilizations.*

None of this is to suggest that the above initiatives represent a full-fledged application of dialogical perspectives to the theory and practice of citizenship. The wider normative framework envisaged here will not emerge easily or painlessly. Citizenship inspired by the dialogical ethic will require individuals and the various communities to which they belong to come to terms with the difficult task of reconciliation. Many communities have suffered from past violence, and some continue to suffer today. Yet, we also know that many of these same communities have been the perpetrators of violence. The new citizenship will require of those steeped in different religious and cultural traditions to share their (hi)stories and to listen to one another's experience of pain, to acknowledge past wrongs, and to assume collective responsibility for righting the wrongs of the past. Civilizational dialogue can become a force for healing to the extent that it nurtures a radical ethic in the evolving organization of human affairs. The implications for both states and international organizations, including the UN, the IMF or the WTO, are equally far-reaching. These institutions have a tendency to appropriate normative and ethical ideas and symbols as much in the support of the rich as of the poor. Official rhetoric is often used to find favor with powerful constituencies, be they domestic or international. The new citizenship will have to subject all formal structures to probing scrutiny.

The preceding analysis offers no more than a map for the possible trajectory of civilizational dialogue. Such a possibility may or may not materialize. Whether or not it does will greatly depend on two equally important and interdependent variables: the extent to which the state allows the voices of civil society sufficient political space to express themselves, and conversely the extent to which the discursive practices of civil society can draw upon the deepest civilizational insights to influence simultaneously the political processes of states, the international rule of law, and the constantly expanding network of regional and global institutions.

References

Beiner, Ronald. 1995. *Theorizing Citizenship.* Albany: State University of New York Press.

Camilleri, Joseph A. 1995. "State, Civil Society, and Economy," in Joseph A. Camilleri, Anthony P. Jarvis, and Albert J. Paolini (eds.), *The State in Transition:*

Reimagining Political Space. Boulder, CO: Lynne Rienner.

Chatterjee, Margaret. 1983. *Gandhi's Religious Thought*. London: Macmillan.

Clarke, Paul Barry, Citizenship, London: Pluto Press, 1994.

Danto, Arthur. 1987. *Mysticism and Morality: Oriental Thought and Moral Philosophy*. Harmondsworth, Middlesex: Penguin Books.

Dods, Marcus, (ed), The Works of Aurelius Augustine, Bishop of Hippo, Vol II: the City of God Edinburgh: T. and T. Clarke, 1871-76.

Friedman, Edward. 1999. "Asia as a Fount of Universal Human Rights," in Peter Van Ness (ed.), *Debating Human Rights: Critical Essays on the United States and Asia*. London: Routledge.

Galtung, Johan. 1993. "International Development in Human Perspective," in John W. Burton (ed.), *Conflict: Human Needs Theory*. London: Macmillan.

Habermas, Jürgen. 1995. "Citizenship and National Identity: Some Reflections on the Future of Europe," in Ronald Beiner (ed.), *Theorizing Citizenship*, pp. 255-282. Albany: State University of New York Press.

Heller, Agnes. "Where Are We at Home?" *Thesis Eleven* 41 (1995): 1-18.

MacPherson, C. B. 1962. *The Political Theory of Possessive Individualism*. London: Oxford University Press.

Marshall, T. H. 1965. Class, *Citizenship and Social Development*. New York: Anchor Books.

Muzaffar, Chandra. 1999. "From Human Rights to Human Dignity," in Peter Van Ness (ed.), *Debating Human Rights: Critical Essays on the United States and Asia*. London: Routledge.

Pollis, Adamantia, and Schwab, Peter (eds.). 1980. *Human Rights: Cultural and Ideological Perspectives*. New York: Praeger.

Said, Abdul Aziz, and Nasser, Jamil. 1980. "The Use and Abuse of Democracy in Islam," in J. L. Nelson and V. M. Green (eds.), *International Human Rights: Contemporary Issues*. Human Rights Publishing Group.

Tai, Hung-Chao. 1985. "Human Rights in Taiwan: Convergence of Two Political Cultures," in James C. Hsiung (ed.), *Human Rights in Asia: A Cultural Perspective*. New York: Paragon House.

Taylor, Charles. 1989. "The Liberal–Communitarian Debate," in N. L. Rosenblum (ed.), *Liberalism and the Moral Life*. Cambridge, MA: Harvard University Press.

Thompson, Kenneth W. (ed.). 1980. *The Moral Imperatives of Human Rights: A World Survey*. Washington, DC: University Press of America for the Council on Religion and International Affairs.

Turner, B. 'Postmodern Culture/Modern Citizens', in Bart van Steenbergen (ed), The Condition of Citizenship, London, Sage, 1994.

Unno, Taitsu. 1988. "Personal Rights and Contemporary Buddhism," in Leroy Rouner (ed.), *Human Rights and the World's Religions*. Notre Dame: University of Notre Dame Press.

Urry, John. "Globalization and Citizenship." *Journal of World-Systems Research* 5 (2) (Spring 1999): 263-273.

Vincent, R. J. 1986. *Human Rights and International Relations*. Cambridge: Cambridge University Press.

Globalization for the Common Good

by Kamran Mofid

Kamran Mofid holds a Ph.D. in economics, and is the Founder of An Inter-faith Perspective on Globalization for the Common Good.
—www.commongood.info

Introduction

Despite many significant achievements since the end of the Second World War in areas such as science, technology, medicine, transportation, and communication, the globalized world economy of today is facing catastrophic socioeconomic, political, cultural, and environmental crises. We are surrounded by global problems of inequality, injustice, poverty, greed, marginalization, exclusion, intolerance, fear, mistrust, xenophobia, terrorism, sleaze, and corruption. These problems are affecting the overall fabric of societies in many parts of the world.

The twentieth century was the bloodiest in human history, with holocausts, genocides, ethnic cleansing, two world wars, and hundreds of inter and intra-national wars. Today, after decades of selfishness, greed, individualism, and emphasis on wealth creation at any cost, the world is entering a period of reflection, self-examination, and spiritual revolution. Many people around the globe have come to an understanding that it is possible to create a better world if a critical mass of people with a sense of human decency and a belief in the ultimate goodness of humanity, rise and realize their power to transform the world. More and more people around the world are finding that there are no short-cuts to happiness. Material wealth is important and this should not be denied. Material wealth, however, is only one ingredient for happiness. Realization of a complete sense of happiness, inner peace, and tranquility can only be achieved through acting more on virtues such as wisdom, justice, ethics, love, and humanity. This spiritual revolution needs architecture and dedicated architects.

Economic Globalization

Globalization, of which we hear so much today, has created an environment and culture in which individual self-interest takes priority over social good. A transactional view of the world dominates economic thinking; personal relationships; and the creation of a stable society is largely ignored in the maximization of profits. This slavish adherence to market forces is wrong and harmful, as it has removed human beings from the equation. Economic globalization, without a globalization of compassion for the common good, is nothing but a house of cards, ready to be blown away by forces that cannot be controlled. The historian Arnold Toynbee (1935), who traced the rise and fall of civilizations, asserted that spirituality was more significant than political leaders in the rise of civilizations, and that once a civilization lost its spiritual core it would sink into decline. As an economist, I believe that the marketplace is not just an economic sphere; it is a region of the human spirit.

Economic questions should, in contrast to what is practiced today, be concerned with the world of heart and spirit. Although self-interest is an important source of human motivation, decisions we make in the marketplace every day, those decisions have a moral, ethical, and spiritual content, because each decision we make affects not only ourselves, but others as well.

As an economist, I appreciate the significance of economics, politics, trade, banking, insurance, and commerce, and of globalization. I understand the importance of wealth creation. But wealth must be created for a noble reason. I want to have a dialogue with the business community. I want to listen to them and be listened to. Today's business leaders are in a unique position to influence what happens in society for years to come. With this power comes monumental responsibility. They can choose to ignore this responsibility, and thereby exacerbate problems such as economic inequality, environmental degradation, and social justice, but this will compromise their ability to do business in the long run. The world of good business needs a peaceful and just world in which to operate and prosper. Future globalization will need to combine economic efficiency with social justice and environmental sustainability to meet human needs.

John Maynard Keynes (1932) predicted a moment when people in advanced economies would step back from traditional economic imperatives and feel free to concentrate on how to live wisely, agreeably, and well. The purpose of the economy, according to Keynes, is to control the material basis of a civilized society, enabling its citizens to explore the higher dimensions of human existence, to discover their own full potential. In our world of prosperity for the few, we seem to have gotten that backwards. Lives are restricted by harsh working conditions and the common assets of a community are degraded in the pursuit of endless economic growth.

In order to arrive at this peaceful and prosperous destination, we need to change the house of neo-classical economics, to make a fit home for the common good. After all, many of the issues that people struggle over, or their governments put forward have, ultimately, economics at their core. Economics once again must find its heart, soul, and spirituality. Moreover, it should also reconnect itself with its original source, rooted in ethics and morality. Today's huge controversy in the economic and business world stems from inadequate attention to the needs of the global collective and the powerless, marginalized, and excluded. This, surely, in the interest of all, has to change. The need for an explicit acknowledgment of true global values, such as altruism, inclusion, universality, fraternity, sympathy, empathy, sharing, security, envisioning, enabling, empowering, solidarity and much more, is the essential requirement in making economics work for the common good. Economics, as practiced today, cannot claim to be for the common good. In short, a revolution in values is needed. The world of economics is sometimes difficult to comprehend, being infused with mathematical jargon, and elaborate economic models and theories, and it has not delivered the happiness that progress has promised because of its failure to satisfy people's spiritual needs. We have to reverse this.

Globalization for the Common Good

Globalization for the common good is an economy of sharing and it is an economy of community. It is not an economy or a system in which well-placed people, institutions, or governments can make a "killing." It is an economy and a philosophy whose aims are generosity and the promotion of a just distribution of God's gifts.

In seeking globalization for the common good, we, the peoples of the world, could together undertake a healing journey, moving from conflict to harmony, achieving the common good in our global home. The economic vision in globalization for the common good is the development of globalization as if people mattered, involving an honest debate on an analysis of integrity, responsibility, accountability, and spirituality for the good of all.

Globalization for the common good will ensure the success of globalization because it will remember that the marketplace is not only a place of trade; it is also a region for the human spirit, for love and compassion. The practice of business and formulation of economics is generally carried out with little or no reference to spiritual concerns. My own recent work has focused on the need to re-introduce these values into the world of commerce (Mofid 2002, 2003, 2005). I have realized, after twenty-five years of teaching economics, that only a spiritually and philosophically committed mind will strive for humane globalization, for ethical as well as corporate social responsibility. If there is no humanity and spirituality, no love, then the laws enforcing business ethics and corporate responsibility will be broken in the selfish interests of profit-seeking, by the few, for the few. Globalization for the common good is all about commitment and hope. It is a challenge for hearts and minds. It meets bad ideas with better ones, disadvantage with imagination and vision.

Globalization for the common good empowers us with humanity, spirituality, and love. It will raise us above pessimism to an ultimate optimism; turning from darkness to light; from night to day; from winter to spring. This spiritual ground for hope at this time of wanton destruction of our world, can help us recognize the ultimate purpose of life and of our journey in this world.

The Essential Dimensions of Globalization for the Common Good:

The acknowledgement of God, Ultimate Reality, or the One. Our lives are grounded in an Ultimate Reality, the source of the sacredness of all life and of the spiritual power, hope, and trust that we discover in prayer or meditation, in word or silence, and in our striving for just relationships with all existence.

The investment of Spiritual Capital. The most powerful way for faith and spiritual communities to influence beliefs, norms and institutions is through prophetic voice and public action. Highly visible faith and interfaith affirmation of the great spiritual truths of peace, justice, and the sacredness of the Earth and all life can make a tremendous contribution to Globalization for the Common Good. Action and service by spiritual and faith communities and groups can provide a vital source of inspiration and energy for the healing of the world.

The practice of selfless Love. The most important point of convergence shared by the world's great spiritual traditions is to be found in the practice and power of selfless love for all humanity. It is the wellspring of the best hope for a better future.

The cultivation of interfaith Dialogue and Engagement. It is absolutely vital that religious and spiritual communities come together with one another in honest and open dialogue. It is also essential that these communities enter into dialogue with secular groups, organizations and governments working for a better world. Religious and spiritual communities – in mutual respect and partnership – must engage the critical issues that face the planetary community as the 21ˢᵗ century unfolds.

The nurturing of cultures of Peace. True cultural evolution is perhaps best measured in the growing rejection of violent approaches to conflict resolution in favour of the cultivation of the infrastructures of forgiveness, reconciliation and peace. Our greatest contribution to the future lies in ensuring that our children grow to maturity in cultures of peace.

The struggle for Justice. Justice is the heart of all creation. It is the profound feeling of oneness with all other beings in the universe. Today, it finds its most vital expression in social and economic fairness, concern for others and the vigorous defence of human rights.

The realization of Gender Partnership. Challenging the assumptions and infrastructures of patriarchy is essential to cultural evolution. Women and men, living and working together in harmony and equity, can build stronger, more creative religious communities and societies.

The path of Sustainability. In this rapidly changing world, our reverence for the Earth will determine the fate of the entire community of planetary life. This deep, visionary and unconditional caring for what is yet to come, is the love of life embedded in ecological sustainability.

The commitment to Service. Service is our link to spirit. Personal action for a better world is the discernable manifestation of the divine in the human. The essence of service is the grace of giving. We give because giving is how life begins and how it continues. This process will enhance personal responsibility for the common good.

Globalization for the Common Good affirms that economics is, above all, concerned with human well-being and happiness in society and with care for the Earth. This cannot be separated from moral and spiritual considerations. The idea of a "value-free" economics is spurious. It demonstrates a complete misunderstanding of what it means to be a human being.

We affirm our conviction that genuine interfaith dialogue and cooperation is a significant way of bringing the world together. It is indispensable to the creation of the harmonious global culture needed to build peace, justice, sustainability and prosperity for all. The call for Globalization for the Common Good is an appeal to our essential humanity. It engages the most pressing concerns of peoples the world over.

In all, Globalization for the Common Good, by addressing the crises that face us all, empowers, enables and envisions us with humanity, spirituality and love. It engages people of different races, cultures and languages, from a wide variety of backgrounds, all committed to bringing about a world in which there is more solidarity and greater harmony. This spiritual ground for hope at this time of wanton destruction of our world, can help us to recall the ultimate purpose of life and of our journey in this world.

Achieving Globalization for the Common Good

If we truly want to change the world for the better, all of us, the business community, politicians, workers, men and women, young and old, must truly become better ourselves. We must share a common understanding of the potential for each one of us to become self-directed, empowered, and active in defining this time in the world as an opportunity for positive change and healing. We can achieve a culture of peace by giving thanks, spreading joy, sharing love and understanding, seeing miracles, discovering goodness, embracing kindness and forgiveness, practicing patience, teaching tolerance, encouraging laughter, celebrating and respecting the diversity of cultures and religions and peacefully resolving conflicts. We must each of us become an instrument of peace.

In short, in the words of Mahatma Gandhi (1925), we should declare ourselves against the "Seven Social Sins." These are:

- Politics without principles
- Commerce without morality
- Wealth without work
- Education without character
- Science without humanity
- Pleasure without conscience
- Worship without sacrifice.

Moreover, in the words of Robert Muller (1997), former UN Under-Secretary General, we ought:

To see the world with global eyes;

To love the world with a global heart;

To understand the world with a global mind;

To merge with the world with a global spirit.

We can achieve this by:

- bringing the material consumption of our species into balance with the needs of the earth;
- realigning our economic priorities so that all persons have access to an adequate and meaningful means of earning a living for themselves and their families;

- democratizing our institutions to route power to people and communities;
- replacing the dominant culture of materialism with cultures grounded in life-affirming values of cooperation, caring, compassion, and community;
- integrating the material and spiritual aspects of our beings so that we become whole persons.

Our task for the future of globalization is to create an "ecumenical space" for dialogue among civilizations, and the building of community for the common good that brings economics, spirituality, and theology together (Mofid 2002, 2003).

References

Gandhi, Mahatma. 1925. "Seven Social Sins." *Young India.* http://www.mkgandhi.org/FAQ/q8.htm (accessed May 20, 2005).

Keynes, John Maynard. 1932. "Economic Possibilities for Our Grandchildren." In Essays *of Persuasion.* New York: Harcourt, Brace and Co.

Mofid, Kamran and Marcus Braybrooke. 2005. Promoting the Common Good: Bringing Economics and Threology Together Again. London: Shepeard-Walwyn.

Mofid, Kamran. 2002. *Globalisation for the Common Good.* London: Shepheard-Walwyn.

Mofid, Kamran. 2003. *Business Ethics, Corporate Social Responsibility and Globalization for the Common Good.* London: Shepheard-Walwyn.

Muller, Robert, and Gaughen, Barbara. 1997. *The Third Five Hundred Ideas of Two Thousand Ideas for a Better World.* http://www.robertmuller.org/voladnl/v3adnl.htm (accessed May 20, 2005).

Toynbee, Arnold. 1935. *A Study of History.* London: Oxford University Press.

Rethinking Civilization: Communication and Terror in the Global Village

by Majid Tehranian

Majid Tehranian is the director of the Toda Institute for Global Peace and Policy Research. This is the text of a lecture given on March 24, 2005, to the Soka Gakkai International in Kuala Lumpur, Malaysia. It summarizes the author's forthcoming book of the same title.

Good evening, my good friends! I am delighted to be among you. I have talked to my Soka Gakkai friends in many world cities, including New York, Los Angeles, Chicago, London, Florence, Frankfurt, Durban, and Istanbul. You are the harbingers of a new civilization, global in scope, sustained by global citizens such as yourselves. You have taken up a new responsibility that others have so far shirked. Our Planet Earth is a fragile place. It is threatened by over-population, depletion of resources, environmental pollution, weapons of mass destruction, tribalism, and terrorism. If we are to save ourselves from extinction as human species, in addition to our local and national citizenships, we have to assume global responsibility. Based upon your Buddhist faith, you have done so. I wish to sincerely congratulate you.

I also wish to take up the subject of Civilization with you tonight. It is a daunting subject. I will be standing on the shoulders of such giants as Lao Tzu (roughly 500 BCE), Jalal ed-Din Rumi (1207-1273), Ibn Khaldun (1332-1406), Niccolo Machiavelli (1469-1527), Giambattista Vico (1668-1744), Edward Gibbon (1737-1794), Alexis De Tocqueville (1805-1859), Karl Marx (1818-1883), Max Weber (1864-1920),

Arnold Toynbee (1884-1975), Mahatma Gandhi (1869-1948), and many others who have dared to write about the subject.

I will be assuming a new approach suited to our own era. In fact, I will have to redefine the term "civilization" in order to make my point. As you know, the term has been often employed to make a distinction between "us" versus "them," the civilized versus the barbarians. I am going to argue that there is no "us" versus "them" any more. We are passengers on the same ship, the *Planet Earth*. Our planet is whirling in a vast and endless space that as far as we can see shows no signs of life except what we witness here on earth. The first astronauts that circled the earth gave us a glimpse of what this means by transmitting pictures of a throbbing blue planet that we call our home (see the photographs of the earth from space). Scientists such as James Lovelock later proposed a hypothesis called the Gaia Hypothesis, named after the Greek myth of Mother Earth. Lovelock argues that the Planet Earth appears as an organism with all of its features. It breathes, it inhales, it secretes, it gets to be sick, it recovers, it lives, it ages, and it may someday die. What we do as inhabitants of this organic whole contributes to its illness or well-being. If we pollute too much, Mother Earth will fall victim to its consequences. Over-population would result in scarcities and wars. If we employ weapons of mass destruction, it will wipe out important elements of the balance sustaining life. As far as our human consciousness can take us, we are not innocent bystanders. Yet, we often act thoughtlessly without attention to the consequences of our own actions.

How should we re-conceptualize "Civilization" to account for the new consciousness of oneness? Ever since the Enlightenment in the eighteenth century, many European thinkers started to think of civilization as something that happened in Europe. Europe thus assumed the responsibility to transport it to other parts of the world. Some called it a "White Man's Burden." They conceived of civilization as a process of linear progress. Economists argued that this is essentially a process of economic growth. The classical economists argued that get the government out of the market and the economic forces eventually through free trade will create a world of plenty for everyone. But Karl Marx came along and argued that left to itself, the market will create pockets of riches and oceans of poverty. So he re-conceptualized the notion of civilization and progress as a movement from primitive communism to ancient slave societies, feudalism, capitalism, and finally to socialist and communist revolutions. Marx was heavily influenced by another theorist, Charles Darwin, who had studied the same progress in nature. And then more recently, in 1960, Walt Rostow published a book called *The Non-communist Manifesto*. His idea was that linear progress will take place along tradition, pre-take off, and take-off into self-sustaining growth and high mass consumption. He used the imagery of a jet plane taking off. Take-off into self-sustained growth was followed by high mass consumption. This metaphor resembled what happened in American society. Every family will have at least two automobiles, but they will all suffocate in traffic and pollution. Daniel Bell (1973) followed the argument by proposing the idea of a post-industrial, information society. In all these conceptions of civilization, the idea of a linear and inevitable progress persisted.

The other view of civilization, which was a bit more pessimistic, could be called cyclical. Spengler, the German scholar who wrote a book, *The Decline of the West*, popularized the concept of the West in international discourse. But he also argued that civilizations like human organisms are born, develop, decline, and die. Toynbee took the cyclical idea a little further and identified twenty-seven dead and living civilizations in history. To Toynbee, they all seemed to have gone through an organic process of birth, development, decline, and death. An Indian scholar by the name of Sarkar took the caste system in India as a metaphor for cyclical patterns in human civilization. He argued that each stage of civilization is led by a different caste—the military, the bureaucrats, the intellectuals, and the businessmen.

What distinguishes us from the rest of the animal kingdom? For instance, what distinguishes an architect from a honeybee? A honeybee is a wonderful engineer, but it replicates the same patterns of honeycombs over and over again. The architect, on the other hand, is not necessarily as precise an engineer as the honeybee. But architects are very imaginative honeybees. They produce a whole variety of buildings. Look at Kuala Lumpur. I am very impressed by some of your marvelous high-rise buildings. So, imagination is central in human beings. We are naturally visionary, that is to say we are spiritual beings. We aspire beyond ourselves. And we do so under the power of our imagination. Civilization is one of those aspirations and imaginaries.

If we define civilization as the pursuit of peace with peaceful means, it would be an unfinished journey. We all are civilized and barbarians at the same time. Take a young American soldier who, after having gone to church every Sunday and having been told "Thou shalt not kill," is sent to the Iraqi frontline with a machine gun facing a hidden and unknown enemy. He uses his machine gun for survival and out of fear. He is neither civilized nor uncivilized. The context brings barbarism out of him. Witness the atrocities at the Abu Gharib prison. In his own church, the soldier is very civilized on Sundays. In Baghdad, with a machine gun, he is very barbaric. So the conditions imposed upon us dictate certain behaviors.

Civilization is a journey, number one. It is not finished. It is a movement toward peace with peaceful means. I realize that we have here a normative construction. Human society is generally a normative construction. Concepts such as "freedom," "democracy," and "friendship" are all normative concepts. They are moral visions that bring about humane societies in human gatherings. In certain respects, we are making considerable progress but, in certain other respects, we are regressing. As technologies of warfare have improved, hit-kill ratios have also changed. With nuclear weapons today, we can kill masses of people, whereas with a little arrow you could kill only one sentient being. Is this progress?

We have progressed technologically. Have we progressed morally? That is a question that I like to pose. Instead of thinking about civilization in linear terms or as organic cycles, let's think of it as layers. At one of the archaeological sites in the Middle East, I was told by our archaeological guide that I was looking at twenty-seven layers of human settlement. That seems to me a more historically accurate way of looking at civilization.

Here in South East Asia we have layers upon layers of civilization. You have Orang Asli, the Malay pre-Sultanate tradition, the Malay Sultanate tradition, followed by the British colonial tradition. Some of the systems today are borrowed from the British colonial period. Then you have the post-Independence tradition. At the same time, you have the Chinese, Indian, and the Malay-Islamic influences. A correct understanding of your very complex society is to think of it in terms of these layers upon layers. Rather than as progression towards some concept of technological and moral progress or some kind of cyclical recurrence, the layering metaphor makes a little more sense to me.

If you accept this notion, the next question will be what kind of layering is universal? Can we talk about a universal layering of human civilization? I should say yes, you can. This morning I spent some time at your museum and I found some evidence for my theory. I found evidence that we have had in history five major technological breakthroughs. We started as hunters and gatherers, maybe five hundred thousand years ago here in South East Asia, then we moved on to the invention of agriculture, the idea that you can till the land and get fruit out of it. It happened around river basins: to name just a few, the Euphrates, the Tigris, and the Nile. Once you filled up your own stomach, you started producing surplus food that you wished to exchange for something you did not have. In Eurasia, we see the development of huge trade routes that came to be known as the Silk Road, the Spice Route, and the Incense Road. The Straits of Malacca became one of the central passageways through which great international trade took place, particularly from the sixteenth century onward.

We may call this the commercial civilization. It created money, banking, and credit. Today we call it capitalism. Capitalism was invented here in Eurasia, the travel between China and Rome and all the passageways along the way. From the sixteenth to the eighteenth centuries, we witnessed the rise of a new type of civilization led by a new mega-technological breakthrough which we call industrial. It began with the printing press in the fifteenth century; it culminated with the rise of steam-powered energy of James Watt in the eighteenth century. Industrial civilization is now penetrating China and Southeast Asia.

But we also have technological leapfrogging. From the 1970s onward we have seen a new phenomenon led by the telecommunications industry. With the invention of the micro-chip, a new Digital Civilization is reducing all communication to zeroes and ones—the digital revolution. Print, film, television, cable, voice, data, and images are all converging. This revolution is making an enormous impact on every aspect of life, in education, government, services, and beyond. If you could see the world in this light, you would understand the conflicts in Iraq and in Afghanistan differently. As you can see it on your television screens, this is an encounter between a digital civilization in North America and a nomadic-agrarian civilization in Afghanistan and Iraq.

We now have at least five different belief systems, five different economic, political, and cultural foundations of society. The conflict obviously is for the hearts, minds, and resources of the world. If you look at the world in this framework, it will begin to open up new insights, new possibilities and challenges for peace. First, we live in a highly uneven world. Since the sixteenth century when European societies began to take off, the world has become increasingly uneven. That unevenness in the

economy, in the polity, and the culture of the world is leading inevitably to serious conflicts.

Secondly, to reduce conflict, we need to narrow these gaps. How can we do it? For one thing, we need more dialogue among civilizations. Dialogue begins with listening. That means trying to understand the Palestinians, to understand the Chechnyans, to understand the Afghans, and to understand the Tibetans. In other words, we need to understand those sectors of the world society that have been silenced by oppression, repression, or historical lags. Without understanding you cannot do anything. And understanding means understanding by the mind as well as the heart.

So if that is the conclusion, then, what does it mean for you and for me as individuals? Well, this is not the first time that we have faced the challenge, although this round we are facing it with greater intensity. Weapons of mass destruction have left no us and them. We are in the same boat, all of us. If there is going to be a nuclear holocaust it is going to have worldwide consequences. It all depends on which way the wind blows the radioactive materials. If something happens in New York, it affects Malaysia. If something happens in Afghanistan, it affects Honolulu. But this is not the first time. It happened earlier along the Eurasian Silk, Spice, and Incense Roads. Out of Central Asia, a poet emerged in the thirteenth century who gave us the answer. His name was Rumi. He has been translated extensively into English. Here is what he said:

What shall I say, O'Muslims?
I know not myself.
I am neither a Christian, nor a Jew,
Nor a Zoroastrian, nor a Muslim.
Neither of the East, nor of the West,
Nor of the desert, nor of the sea

Neither from the land, nor of the sky.
Neither of the earth, nor of water,
Nor of wind, nor of fire.
Neither of the high, nor of low,
Nor of space, nor of time,
Neither an Indian, nor Chinese
Nor Bulghar, nor Saksin
Neither of Iraq, nor of Khorasan
Neither of this world, nor of the next
Nor of paradise, nor of hell.
Neither of Adam, nor of Eve
My Place is the placeless
My sign is the signless
There is neither a body nor a soul.
For I am of the Beloved.

That was Rumi in the thirteenth century. But another man said something of equal relevance to our own times. His name is Daisaku Ikeda. In September 1996, he said, "I wish people could be like the water lilies, bloom untainted in a muddy world."

Reference

Bell, Daniel. The Coming of Post-Industrial Society: A Venture in Social Forecasting. New York, NY: Basic Books, 1973 & 1999. (see attachment pls)

Process Theology and Ecology in the Age of Globalization

by Christopher A. Leeds

Christopher A. Leeds was formerly member of the Council of the Conflict Research Society, London, a visiting research fellow at the University of Kent at Canterbury (2000-2001), and researcher at the University of Nancy 2, France since 2002.

Introduction

This article explores aspects of the themes of Christianity, ecology, and globalization in Process Theology. Christianity, Judaism, and Islam belong to the same roots, historically. These three monotheistic religions emphasize a transcendent God (theism). Confucianism, and a number of other religions are largely "human-based," which seek ultimate good through harmonization. Theology applies ideas from philosophy and culture not confined to Christianity. Within this pluralistic discipline people of different beliefs can cooperate and converse together (Ward 1994: 45).

Process thought reflects the thinking of philosophers, for example, Heraclitus, Leibniz, Bergson, James, and Whitehead, from which sources Process Theology derives as a branch of Christianity.[1] Process Theology developed originally in North America associated with Protestantism, but also finds adherents among Roman Catholic and Jewish thinkers (Vertin 1987: 45). It has an offshoot in Liberation Theology. One study focuses on the respective potential of the thinking of Hegel and Whitehead, respectively, as supports in relation to Liberation Theology (Lakeland 1986). A variation, Black Liberation Theology, is associated with the thoughts of Afro-Americans.[2]

A final section discusses the growth of shared outlooks in certain religious/spiritual areas between Western process thinkers and representatives of Buddhism in the East, a trend associated with a form of globalization.

Worldviews

Greek philosophy and Christianity emphasize the idea of substance as the static essence of things, an interpretation that influenced perceptions of both the material world and God. Before quantum physics, the scientific view interpreted the universe as a mindless machine that consisted of entities subject to mechanical laws.

Quantum Theory was discovered in the 1920s by a group of physicists, including Max Planck and Albert Einstein. Bohr (1934) argues that isolated material particles are abstractions, their properties only definable and observable through interaction with other systems. The universe now appears to comprise a multitude of objects, the parts of a cosmic process interrelating within one indivisible, dynamic whole. This interpretation, whereby all objects are mere processes, rather than consisting of material substance, has long been accepted in the East, notably in Buddhist and Chinese thought (Capra 1992: 226). Easterners tend to interpret the universe as a multidimensional, living organism. In the West, the static interpretation of the world of classical philosophy and theology has now been replaced by the perception that the world is in process.

Worldviews encapsulate the notion of major ways of thinking. The Western worldview (WV) tends to interpret life as a competitive struggle and belief in continual, material progress. The WV of the East, organic holism, provides a closer vision of how the earth and the universe interact than the Western WV. Quantum mechanics appears to demonstrate the complementarity of both secular science and spiritual traditions. Some physicists demonstrate a link between developments in quantum physics and certain non-Western, intuitive holistic worldviews such as Buddhism and Taoism (Le Shan 1982).

Process Thinking, Process Theology

Whitehead (1929) added to quantum physics by developing a particular vision of the universe, the world, the role of God, and interpretation of how humans and other entities fitted into the model. Whitehead identified a metaphysical system of live bursts of energy, which he called experiences. The nature of the world could only be explained by the existence of God who was present in each experience. The term "feeling" is used by Whitehead to indicate both the way a new moment of experience recalls experiences of the past and how each pulse of experience constitutes a harmonizing of past feelings through a process of complex, synthetic unification.

Whitehead was influenced by the ideas of Hegel and by Leibniz (1646-1716), a Prussian scientist and philosopher who believed that the universe contained an infinite number of monads. The latter are arranged in an ascending scale from simple monads in rocks to complex monads, with God at the top, human beings being somewhere in the middle. Whitehead called monads "actual occasions" or events. As each event perishes, it establishes a creative advance into the future by passing on new information to immediate successors. Such events are co-ordinated and held together by the primordial nature of God. The process view of God has become popular among many Christians, probably because God persuades by love, patience, encouragement, and companionship rather than as a dominating tyrant (Ward 2003).

Following Whitehead, Process thinkers tend to interpret the role of God as pantheistic, one which both transcends and is immanent in the world (Barbour 2000: 35). Based on ideas associated with Whitehead and his followers, Process Theology provides both a religiously sensitive alternative to anthropocentrism and modernity's cosmic pessimism. Process Theology interprets God's role as persuasive rather than coercive, which lures the cosmos, at every stage of its evolution, in the manner of love rather than force, towards new and richer forms of order (Haught 2000: 227-228).

Process Theology constitutes one of the forms of Western thought that shares qualities with Buddhism. Christian theologians, for example, John Cobb, stress the importance of relational processes over substances, which is close to Buddhist dependent becoming.[3] A Buddhist visualizes the self in process-relational terms. The latter shares affinities with communitarianism, by which individuals are embedded in communities. This contrasts with the atomic individualism or "external relatedness" of liberalism (Kakol 2000).

Process Thought in the West shares certain qualities with Eastern thinking. The fact that process thought generally characterizes aspects of Chinese and Buddhist holistic cultures facilitates contacts. Process Thinking possesses a theological wing across Christian denominations and a record of dialogue across religions, especially with Japanese Buddhism, and to a lesser extent with Chinese Buddhism (Moses 2000).

According to Bitner, Whitehead provides no doctrine of Scripture, of Christ, the Holy Spirit, or of eschatology, merely the doctrine of God.[4] In addition, Whitehead believes in a God that is constantly changing rather than the God of orthodox understanding, immutable, omnipresent, omniscient, and omnipotent.[5] Whitehead's God rests in a state of flux whereas the Bible reveals that God remains unchanging throughout eternity.

The deity of Whitehead's philosophical synthesis is completely incompatible with God as revealed in the Bible. The Scriptures state clearly that the route to salvation passes by Christ (John 14:6). The biblical view of Christ interprets the Redeemer as absolutely necessary for the salvation of man. Process Theology, rather than being true theology, is merely a humanistic philosophy disguised as theology. Bitner argues that Bible-believing Christians must oppose such an interpretation of God.

Despite the criticisms of Process Theology, God can be interpreted according to a liberal interpretation of the Bible. That the world has been undergoing a process of constant change since the beginning of Time is incontestable. If God is really omnipotent, he can also share other characteristics that concord with Process Theology.

Bahá'u'lláh, born in Persia in 1817, founded the Bahá'i Faith. His vision of the world shares characteristics associated with Whitehead and process theologians. Bahá'u'lláh argued that Man has developed over a period of time and, in the process of evolution and progressive revelation, has passed through many different forms. The unseen force of God is all around us, in nature, in man himself, and in history. The Bahá'i community aims to build a new world civilization of harmony and peace in which there will be opportunity for spiritual growth and fulfillment for all, free from the oppression of hatred, prejudice, violence, and injustice (Huddleston 1976).

The Environment and Ecological Issues

Environment (nature) covers the complete range of physical and biological conditions around us. Humans and other organisms, such as trees, plants, and animals, cannot survive outside a particular environment. Ecology involves the study of animals, plants, balance, harmony, and interrelatedness within a particular environment (Gnanakan 1999: 2-3).

A wide range of religious and spiritual traditions endorse values such as humility, love for others, and respectful treatment of all beings. Reinterpreting Christianity ecocentrically is the concern of eco-theology. Christian teachings in the Sermon on the Mount share much in common with spiritual traditions that teach respect for all life forms (Drengson 2001). Many religions interpret the natural world as a source for teaching, visionary inspiration, revelation, food, and clothing. Religions have created complex systems of exchange and thanksgiving based on human dependence on animals, plants, forests, and rivers. Religious ecology provides understanding of how people and cultures create symbolic systems of human-earth relations and practical means of maintaining such relations (Tucker and Grim 2001: 15-16).

Individualists frequently adopt a minimalist, moralist approach to major issues such as the environment. They show, in general, little concern for non-human entities such as animals or forests (Midgley 2002: 38-39). The mainstream Western ethic highlights humankind as the only significant living species. As a result of their elevated position among life forms, many Westerners reason that humans should dominate the natural world and adopt an instrumental approach to the environment. Nature provides a source of gratification, to be manipulated and controlled (Doran 1995: 202).

The global environmental crisis has been associated notably with Western industrialization and development. An important number of Christians believed that God willed that humans could exploit nature for their own purposes (White 1967: 1205). According to this anthropocentric interpretation, God gave man the stewardship of the earth.[6] This viewpoint has been challenged in the United States. During the formative years of American history since the arrival of Europeans, both capitalist and environmental matters were taken into account. Americans led the world in terms of measures implemented to reduce pollution, develop parks, and enforce wildlife protection (Stoll 1997: ix-x). Pollution, as a result of industrialization, has been a problem in parts of the East, for example, Thailand and China.

Two movements, Shallow Ecology and Deep Ecology, represent two responses to the environmental crisis. The former considers only human interests and handling environmental problems within the limits of the current Western worldview, while making certain modifications in technology, behavior, and policy, such as recycling. In contrast, Deep Ecology respects all life forms on earth, including humans, and advocates the replacement of an anthropocentric worldview by an earth-centered (anthropocosmic) worldview that facilitates ecological sustainability, and in which humans form part of the cosmic order. This second approach, a nature-centered view (ecocentric), rejects the instrumental value of nature (Naess 1989).

Process Theology reflects a broad metaphysical vision, a feature that is shared with the Deep Ecology movement (Moses 2000: 1). Whereas Process Theology focuses particularly on the wider cosmos, eco-theology specializes on the environmental concerns of this world. Humans achieve peace with God by making peace with nature. Various developments, such as the growth of eco-feminism and the animal rights movement, challenge the traditional Christian outlook regarding non-human nature. Deep ecology visualizes earth as a total system in which the human dimension is in symbiosis with the non-human but life-centered dimension. Every existing thing represents one actual expression of the universe's infinitely unfolding potentiality, according to quantum field theory (Zohar 1997: 127-128).

Whitehead never used the term "postmodern" but the notion is implicit in a book he wrote in 1925, *Science and the Modern World*. He argues that recent developments in physics and philosophy have replaced some of the scientific and philosophical ideas that were the basis for understanding the modern world. Many postmodern process theologians challenge patriarchy, reject divine power, and support both ecological and feminist liberation in the aim of liberating the planet from modern economism (perpetual economic growth), which has undermined communities, destroyed the environment, and widened the rich-poor divide (Daly and Cobb 1994).

Concern increased during the 1980s over deforestation, since tropical forests help to absorb excess carbon dioxide, 80 percent of which is caused by industrialized countries. A General Agreement on Tariffs and Trade (GATT) study on Trade and Environment, prepared for the Earth Summit at Rio de Janeiro in 1992, maintains that countries with large rain forests should get financial compensation for "carbon absorption services." The report made no mention of the need for Northern countries to restructure consumption patterns. President George Bush, Sr., on the eve of the Earth Summit, expressed little interest in the environment. "The American way of life is not negotiable," he declared (Khor 1992: 2). The implication is that the West can continue to exploit the environment.

The Declaration of the Sacred Earth Gathering of Spiritual Leaders, UNCED Conference, Rio de Janeiro, 1992, warned that Planet Earth is in serious peril. Educators were urged to motivate people towards living in harmony with nature and all life forms, and to curtail impulses of greed, consumerism, and the disregard of natural laws. After the 1992 Earth Summit, years of negotiation led to no positive results on global warming. However, the twentieth century recorded the highest temperatures in 1,000 years. Many scientists believe that a link exists between global warming and the increase in natural disasters such as droughts, storms, and floods. Most experts feel that the main problem, greenhouse gas emissions, results from human activities, of which Western nations are the chief culprits. Global warming worsens the imbalance between North and South since the

greatest impact falls on poor countries, the least able to cope.[7]

Nature's resources are finite. Through industrialization, including exploitation of natural resources and the resultant pollution caused by toxic industrial products, development contributes to both the destruction of eco-systems (air, soil, forest, and water degradation) and the extinction of bio-diversity. Humanity faces the risk of climatic changes, ozone depletion, and other degradations in the earth's capacity to support forms of life. Necessary changes to avert this eventuality include changing destructive technologies, lifestyles, and ourselves (George 1995: 136-137).

Among various environmental hazards, greenhouse gases, caused by burning coal and oil are the main problem. Energy use is the primary human activity responsible for global warming, which accounts for about 50 percent of all greenhouse emissions. Various actors involved in environmental matters include corporate decision-makers, local authorities, energy companies, individuals, environmental pressure groups, and grass root global organizations such as the Social Justice and Appropriate Technology Movement.

Radical environmentalists, who promote an ecological consciousness, defend terrorist activities as the only means of preventing possibly irretrievable damage to the global ecological system by businesses or governments. An example was the act of ecological sabotage by the Earth Liberation Front (ELF) in Colorado (1998) against a large ski operator, which prioritized profits rather than the preservation of wildlife. Radical environmentalism can be traced to the deep ecology movement which maintains that non-human life possesses a special value (Sim 2004: 204-205). Radical ecologists believe that modernity has not been in the best interests of the planet. Extreme proponents of deep ecology advocate turning the clock back to a pre-industrial society so as to minimize damage to the earth. Ecologically based arguments have become significant in relation to critiques of neo-liberal globalization. One proposal favors collective action and the development of global forms of democratic authority as a means of preventing ecological catastrophe (Gill 1995: 41).

The philosophical and spiritual basis of deep ecology has been highlighted at various periods in the past by thinkers such as the Taoist Huai Nan Tzu, Heraclitus, Saint Francis, and Spinoza. Since the 1970s, many individuals and groups have moved from material consumption preoccupations to an inner growth lifestyle. A study by Stanford Research Institute in 1976 estimated that about 14 million Americans embraced some or all of the tenets of the voluntary simplicity approach, notably frugal consumption, ecological awareness, and concern with inner growth (Capra 1992: 458-460). Such trends also occurred in Europe and parts of Asia where people, to an extent, follow practices embedded in Taoist and Buddhist traditions.

East-West Dialogue and Focus on Complementary Values

Taoism rejects self-assertiveness, competition, and materialism, while emphasizing simplicity of life and union with nature. Happiness occurs when a person acts spontaneously and trusts her/ his own intuition. In the eleventh century, the Neo-Confucian school developed a form of synthesis of Confucianism, Taoism and Buddhism (Capra 1992: 113-114). In East Asia, a number of religions are largely philosophical and spiritually oriented. As a result, a person may be attached to a number of spiritual faiths or religions. For example, a person may possess the peace of mind of a Buddhist, taking care of his body as a Taoist, and remaining a good citizen as a Confucian.

Siddhartha Gautama, the founder of Buddhism in the sixth century BC, believed that knowledge, derived from the intellect or the conscious mind, continually changes. In contrast, the intuitive mind, changeless and permanent, provides a valid guide to absolute reality. Consequently, intuition, not reason, remains the source of ultimate truth and wisdom. Buddhism provides a pattern for living holistically in this world. If a person has a realistic understanding of self as a dynamic, evolving process, this improves adaptability in confronting life situations. The impermanence of life and things must be accepted.[8]

In the early 1970s, John Cobb, Process Theologian, initiated meetings with Abe Masao, Kyoto School Buddhist philosopher, to explore interconnections.[9] Subsequent dialogues led to the formation of the Society for Buddhist and Christian Studies in 1987. One hope is that interactions between representatives of Buddhism and Christianity will culminate in a synthesis between these two religious traditions (Teasdale 1999). The Whitehead and China Conference was held in Beijing, June 2002. In East Asia, the largest Process Society is located in South Korea, where a major conference took place in May 2004.[10] According to Chappell (2003), interfaith dialogue between Christians and Buddhists represents an important step in human religious history.

Science and religion are compatible, process thinking providing some distinctive answers to the classical model of Christianity. Whereas the interpretation of God focused on "masculine" qualities (power, impassability and independence), process thinkers emphasize the importance of "feminine" qualities (nurturing, sensitivity and interdependence). Dialogue and Integration provide more promising ways of linking scientific and religious insights than the paths of Conflict or Independence (Barbour 2000: 179).

Conclusion

The world community has become aware of the need for an all-embracing global ethic for sustainable development, as expressed in The Earth Charter (Weiming 2001: 251). The final version approved by the Earth Charter Commission in Paris, March 12-14, 2000, emphasizes that humanity forms part of an evolving universe that includes an Earth that is alive, possessing a unique life community.

One radical viewpoint in international relations interprets globalization as a state of affairs that retains cultural diversity, traditions, and values. This perspective highlights a "bottom-up" approach to world order based on the importance of self-governing communities and social movements (Held and McGrew 2002: 112-113). This approach to globalization differs from developments in Process Theology that emphasize the growth of shared outlooks between a branch of Protestantism and Asian religions on the nature of process, the merit of embracing a holist orientation, and on ways to handle the present plight of the world.

Notes

1. Alfred Whitehead, born in Ramsgate, Kent, known as both a philosopher and scientist, worked in both the United States and the United Kingdom.
2. http://www.religion-online.org/showarticle.asp?title=2789
3. For Whitehead, God is not the God of the Bible but of the philosopher.
4. Dr. Teddy Bitner is professor at Carolina Bible College, Fayetteville, NC.
5. http://www.ifca.org/voice/99Jul-Aug/Bitner.htm
6. According to certain statements in the Old Testament, for example, Genesis (1.26) (1.28) God allowed man to have dominion over all living things.
7. Michael Bessieres (UNESCO) Courier journalist, "Global Warming: Ignorance is not bliss." *See* http://www.unesco.org/courrier/2001_06/uk/planet.htm.
8. Alfred Bloom, professor emeritus, University of Hawai'i, "Buddhism and Healing," http://www/shindharmanet.com/writings/healing.htm.
9. Cobb is based at Claremont College, Los Angeles. He was, with Charles Hartshorne, one of the original representatives of Process Theology, developing an orientation pioneered by Whitehead.
10. www.alfred.north.whitehead.com. See the International Process Network.

References

Barbour, Ian. 2000. *When Science Meets Religion*. London: Society for Promoting Christian Knowledge.

Bohr, Neils. 1934. *Atomic Physics and the Description of Nature*. London: Cambridge University Press.

Capra, Fritjof. 1992. *The Tao of Physics*, 3rd ed. London: Flamingo.

Chappell, David W. 2003. "Foreword," in Daisaku Ikeda and Majid Tehranian, *Global Civilization: A Buddhist-Islamic Dialogue*, vii-ix. London: British Academic Press.

Daly, Herman E., and Cobb, John. 1994. *For the Common Good: Redirecting the Economy Towards Community, the Environment and a Sustainable Future*. Boston: Beacon.

Doran, Peter. 1995. "Earth, Power Knowledge: Towards a Critical Global Environment Politics," in John MacMillan and Andrew Linklater (eds.), *Boundaries in Question—New Directions in IR*, 193-211. London: Pinter.

Drengson, Alan. "Education for Local and Global Ecological Responsibility: Arne Naess's Cross-Cultural Ecophilosophy Approach." *The Trumpeter* 17 (1) (2001). *See* http://trumpeter.athabascau.ca/ content/v17.1/dregson.html.

George, James. 1995. *Asking for the Earth— Waking up to the Spiritual/ Ecological Crisis*. Shaftesbury: Element Books.

Gill, Stephen. "The Global Panopticon? The Neoliberal State, Economic Life and Democratic Surveillance." *Alternatives* 20 (1) (1995).

Gnanakan, Ken. 1999. *God's World—A Theology of the Environment*. London: SPCK.

Haught, John. 2000. "Theology, Ecology and the Idea of Global Order," in John L. Esposito and Michael Watson (eds.), *Religion and Global Order*, 216-233. Cardiff: University of Wales Press.

Held, David, and McGrew, Anthony. 2002. *Globalization/Anti-Globalization*. Cambridge: Polity Press.

Huddleston, John. 1976. *The Earth is but One Country*. London: Bahá'i Publishing Trust.

Kakol, Peter. "A Socially Engaged Process Buddhism." *Journal of Buddhist Ethics* 7 (2000).

Khor, Martin. "Earth Summit Ends with Disappointment and Hope." *Third World Resurgent* 23 (July 1992).

Lakeland, Paul. "Process and Revolution: Hegel, Whitehead and Liberation Theology." *Process Studies*. 15 (4) (1986): 265-274.

Le Shan, L. 1982. *The Medium, the Mystic and the Physicist: Towards a General Theory of the Paranormal*. New York: Ballantine Books.

Midgley, Mary. 2002. "Individualism and the Concept of Gaia," in Ken Booth, Tim Dunne, and Michael Cox (eds.), *How Might We Live? Global Ethics in the New Century* , 29-44. Cambridge: Cambridge University Press

Moses, James. 2000. "Process Relational Ecological Theology: Problems and Prospects." Paper presented at the ANZATS Conference, Christchurch, New Zealand, July. http://members.optusnet.com.eu/ ~gjmoses/ecoth12k.htm.

Naess, Arne. 1989. *Ecology, Community and Lifestyle: Outline of an Ecosophy*. Trans. and revised by David Rothenberg. New York: Cambridge University Press.

Sim, Stuart. 2004. *Fundamentalist World— The New Dark Age of Dogma*. Cambridge: Icon Books.

Stoll, Mark. 1997. *Protestantism, Capitalism and Nature in America*. Albuquerque: University of New Mexico Press.

Teasdale, Wayne. 1999. *The Mystic Heart: Discovering a Universal Spirituality in the World's Religions*. Novato, CA: New World Library.

Tucker, Mary E., and Grim, John A. "Introduction: The Emerging Alliance of World Religions and Ecology." *Daedalus* 130 (4) (2001): 1-22.

Vertin, Michael. 1987. "Is God in Process?" in Timothy P. Fallon and Philip B. Riley (eds.), *Religion and Culture: Essays in Honour of Bernard Lonergan, S.J.* Albany: State University of New York Press.

Ward, Keith. 1994. *Religious Revelation*. Oxford: Oxford University Press.

Ward, Keith. 2003. *God, a Guide for the Perplexed*. Oxford: One World Publications.

Weiming, Tu. "The Ecological Turn in New Confucian Humanism." *Daedalus* 130 (4) (2001): 243-264.

White, Lynn, Jr. "The Historical Roots of Our Ecologic Crisis." *Science* 155 (3767) (1967): 1203-1207.

Whitehead, Alfred N. 1929 (1985). *Process and Reality—An Essay in Cosmology*. New York: Macmillan.

Zohar, Danah. 1997. *Rewiring the Corporate Brain*. San Francisco: Berrett-Kochler Publishers.

Models of Global Culture

by Vladimir Korobov

Vladimir Korobov, lecturer for Tibetan history, culture and language in the Center of Oriental Studies in Vilnius University, Lithuania.

To what degree can it be said that we are living in a global culture? Where, sitting at my home in Vilnius, Lithuania, can I find signs or traces of global culture? How does global culture represent itself? What is the main problem of global culture?

Global philosopher and former visiting professor at Moscow State University John Naisbitt in his *Global Paradox* describes the situation of equalization, where each man or each women in each country is becoming as the rest of the world: "He wears Ferragamo-designed shirts and ties, sports a Rolex or Cartier watch, has a Louis Vuitton attaché case, signs his signature with a Mont Blanc pen. Goes to work in his flashy BMW, endlessly talks on a mobile Motorola cellular phone, puts all his charges on an American Express card, travels Singapore Airlines, maintains a city apartment, and keeps a country home. He uses Georgio Armani aftershave and buys Poison for his girlfriend. The rising group of affluent Asian career women have wardrobes filled with Christian Dior and Nina Ricci, dressing tables congested with makeup and skin care from Guerlain, YSL and Ester Lauder, shoes from Bruno Magli, wear Chanel No. 5 and jewelry from Tiffany. They both listen to Beethoven's Ninth symphony from their Sony compact disc player either in the car, at home, or in the office" (Naisbitt 1998: 31).

In his book, John Naisbitt describes Asian men and women, but actually at the present time all this is also right for Lithuanian, Latvian, or even Russian men or women. We see here a process of equalization in terms of common goods, trademarks, brands, but do all these attributes of everyday life have anything in common with global culture?

The problem can be restated: What can or should we keep local and what is globalized in the process of globalization? My special interest here concerns the articulation between globalized messages and discourses and local ones. This process always takes place locally in local space (in Lithuania, United States, or China), which is actually symbolic space by its nature, because local and personal symbols here interact with global symbols and symbolic space. From this point of view, I will try to analyze the main functions of global culture or what global culture may be.

Very often global culture is pictured as a kind of "third" culture. According to Featherstone (1996), there exists a global culture that goes beyond the boundaries of any specific nation-state. This is a culture over all national or local cultures.

Featherstone (1995: 6) argues that

...the process of globalization suggests two images of culture. The first image entails the extension outwards of a particular culture to its limit, the globe. Heterogeneous cultures become incorporated and integrated into a dominant culture, which eventually covers the whole world. The second image points to the compression of cultures. The world becomes a singular domesticated space, a place where everyone becomes assimilated into a common culture. A global culture can be considered the culture of the nation-state writ large.

According to Marshall McLuhan the world is a "global village" (McLuhan 1964), where there is a brand-new culture growing. The "global culture" functions as the restricted sense of "third culture": sets of practices, bodies of knowledge, conventions, and lifestyles that are unique cultural phenomena, and have become increasingly independent of any specific nation-state (Featherstone 1996: 60).

The increasing intensity of contacts and communications among cultures is likely to produce the cultural clash, which can lead to heightened attempts to draw boundaries between the self and others (Featherstone 1996: 60). Thus, the intensified globalization process also stimulates reactions among cultural groups who seek to rediscover particularity, localism, and difference. This raises questions about "cultural identity," "national identity," or "collective identity," which are constructed by disadvantaged cultures to resist the invasion of aggressive cultures.

Schlesinger suggested another general concept of "collective identity," which assumed that a group of people shared not only some significant cultural features of ethnicity, language, way of life, etc., but also the same time and place (McQuail 2000: 236). These notions combine "cultural identity" with the idea of "localism," and form a significantly contrary force in the prevailing trend of "globalism." The essence of this contrary force may be represented by the words of culturologist and presenter

David Duke: "The diversity that we must preserve is in the world, in nature. The globalists are attempting to make us all listen to the same music; eat the same food, live the same way. They are the enemies of real diversity, and they are the enemies of freedom. The bigger the government, the less the freedom. How can people in say Zurich decide what is best for people in Kashmir. Real freedom comes from small government, not from a global one. The most important freedom of all is the right to live, and to live as your parents did. We must be able to live in the harmony of our own land and our own culture and our own people." (See: http://www.davidduke.com/radio/transcripts/globalism09042002.htm.)

It has also been broadly discussed that globalism is fundamentally a top-down process, and localism is a bottom-up one (Tehranian 1999: 50). The network of globalization consists of economic and technological facilities that spread around the world, which connect the center of communication to the rest of the network, and negotiate and integrate the competing interests and values of the global players. At the same time, localism plays at its own level, and works through its own networks, which consist of the nationalist, religious, and culturalist movements voicing the peripheries' interests and views (Tehranian 1999: 50). Usually, this complex hybridization cannot be explained as a political "zero-sum games." Most of time, there are no absolute or radical interest conflicts between globalism and localism because they speak at different levels in different languages. Globalism is more an economic process and technological integration, while localism plays on the spiritual, culturalist, and nationalist stages. In this case, global culture is a representation of global economy. We all know that the characteristics of culture have changed due to economic, social, and political factors. The media—the press, broadcasting, as well as the Internet—are accelerating this change, which tends to complicate the relationship between tradition and creativity, between identity and interaction, between the self and the Other.

Improvements in transportation technology now make it possible for like business representatives and executives and wealthy international tourists (i.e., those who can afford it) to traverse the planet within a matter of about a day, radically reducing travel time, which once took weeks or even months. This also means that goods can travel much more quickly between countries. Improved technologies enable quick and efficient businesses. Traders and bankers are able to shift funds, currencies, and other assets between large distances within seconds. Despite that fact, the Internet and email have virtually eliminated borders and times between peoples, and greatly increased the speed with which communication, financial and personal transactions can occur. But the dispersal of these facilities has been very uneven. Ray Kiley (Kiley 1998: 3) reminds us that we need to assess soberly and critically these phenomena:

Much has been made of the potential of the Internet, as a basis for reconstructing and democratising social relations throughout the globe. Although it would be unwise to totally discount the ways that it can be used to rapidly disseminate progressive ideas across the globe, there is still the reality of the massively unequal distribution of communications. At least 80 per cent of the world's population still lacks access to the most basic communications technologies, and nearly 50 countries have fewer than one telephone line per 100 people. There are more telephone lines in Manhattan than there are in the whole of sub-Saharan

Africa. While the United States has 35 computers per 100 people, even rapidly developing South Korea has only 9, while for Ghana the figure is as low as 0.11. Although the number of Internet users has expanded dramatically in recent years, its use is still largely confined to Western Europe and the United States. Moreover, the overwhelming proportion of Internet activity takes place at work. Even if computer prices fall to levels where they become easily affordable, there are other expenses for potential users. These include specialized cabling, advanced modems and online charges. Clearly then, the information superhighway has passed by most of the world's population and is likely to do so for the foreseeable future. This point applies not only to the poorest parts of the so-called Third World, but also to many people living in global cities such as Los Angeles, where new telecommunications networks have produced "electronic ghettoes," in which access is restricted to television screens. Clearly, then, time-space compression is experienced differently across the globe. For the people excluded, this is not even life in the slow lane. It is life on the hard shoulder.

Kiley considers globalization "a world in which societies, cultures, politics and economies have, in some sense, come closer together" (Kiley 1998: 4-5). Jan Nederveen Pieterse argues that we need to look at "globalizations in the plural because there have been globalizations in international relations focusing on the relationships between nation-states; in sociology with talk of "world society" and in cultural studies centering on global communications and world-wide cultural standards such as "Coca-colonisation"; or "McDonaldization" (Pieterse 1995: 45). Indeed, recent developments in communications technology permit, as John Wiseman contends, "the most modern equipment in the Sydney exchange to communicate with a 100-year-old phone box in rural China" (Wiseman 1998: 73).

The world in which we live and which we seek to change to herald the culture of the future is a world composed of a multiplicity of identities or cultures. And so the work for the culture of the future is fraught with a myriad of obstacles and difficulties. It is not possible to determine beforehand such culture, on a global level, or to determine a global cultural model that transcends individual cultures in a world that is still a world of homelands, each of which celebrates its own culture and identity. These homelands, each within the boundaries of their consciousness and aspirations, do not tire of rediscovering their mythologies, their own symbols, their own historical memory, and their own golden ages. Therefore, they fear the obliteration of their national cultures, particularly given that the global economic trend, or rather the nature of the resultant globalism, seems to threaten to obliterate these cultures.

Within this framework, it is necessary to pose the question: does the issue of economic-technological globalism represent a project in preparation for the advent of the culture of the future? Or is it, to the contrary, a project merely to transform the world into a "global village" with one economic market?

There exist then two paradoxical possibilities: the first relates to the elimination of the universalism of the human being in the name of another—false globalism, that of the market. The second is that a country's ability to build itself depends upon having its own distinct cultural character. Moreover, just as it is not possible to preserve identity through repression, tyranny, and isolationism—such as occurs in a number of countries - the erasing of cultural identities through the force of economic-technological globalism would lead to a cultural desertification of the world through the hegemony of the "one culture." It seems that these issues are interrelated: the more market becomes global, the more it requires some common regulation in terms of cultural and ethical norms. These cultural and ethical norms very often conflict with local national cultures hindering the growth of national economy. It is appropriate to introduce here a typology of cultures according to criteria of their nativity. It is possible to mark out three kinds of cultures:

1. national or local cultures,
2. hybrid cultures and
3. global culture.

National or local cultures—nationalism and *hybrid cultures*. Nationalism has been defined by Ernest Gellner as a movement that has aimed at a coincidence between the ethnic community and the political community: one National State, one National Culture has been the political motto of nationalism. The role of nationalism has indeed been the diffusion and popularization of a high written culture that has often replaced a large number of dialects, stratified class idioms and behaviors, and all sorts of traditions. This change has been strictly related to the emergence of industrial societies based on a continuous process of "creative destruction" (Gellner 1998).

According to Samuel P. Huntington, "nation states remain the principal actors in world affairs. Their behavior is shaped as in the past by the pursuit of power and wealth, but it is also shaped by cultural preferences, commonalities, and differences. The most important groupings of states are no longer the three blocs of the Cold War but rather the world's seven or eight major civilizations. Non-Western societies, particularly in East Asia, are developing their economic wealth and creating the basis for enhanced military power and political influence. As their power and self-confidence increase, non-Western societies increasingly assert their own cultural values and reject those 'imposed' on them by the West. The 'international system of the twenty-first century,' Henry Kissinger has noted, '…will contain at least six major powers—the United States, Europe, China, Japan, Russia, and probably India—as well as a multiplicity of medium-sized and smaller countries.' Kissinger's six major powers belong to five very different civilizations, and in addition there are important Islamic states whose strategic locations, large populations, and/or oil resources make them influential in world affairs. In this new world, local politics is the politics of ethnicity; global politics is the politics of civilizations. The rivalry of the superpowers is replaced by the clash of civilizations" (Huntington 1998: 21-22).

The definition that would be accepted by most parties in the debate today is that a nation is a cultural group, possibly, but not necessarily united by a common descent, endowed with some kind of civic ties (Seymour 2000).

Hybrid cultures. It would be entirely incorrect to suggest that smaller countries, cultures, and consumers blindly adopt and accept American- (and European) generated cultural artifacts and identities. In most cases, these "local" cultural consumers fuse their own identities with the "global" products and construct "hybrid" ("foreign + local") forms of culture and identities.

Throughout this century, and indeed especially after World War II, an American "culture," and, to a lesser extent, Anglo-American "culture" of capitalist relations, entertainment and sport has penetrated the globe. American-originated consumer artifacts such as McDonald's hamburgers and Pizza Hut pizzas are as highly visible in the streets of Vilnius as they are anywhere in Moscow or Massachusetts. Fans of performers and bands like the Spice Girls, Madonna, Rage Against the Machine, Public Enemy, Metallica, and Pearl Jam are just as easily identifiable in Singapore as they are in their own countries. Arnold Schwarzenegger, Sylvester Stallone, Leonardo DiCaprio, Sharon Stone, Wynona Ryder, Angela Bassett, and Spike Lee all have their films shown regularly throughout the world.

Todd Gitlin has gone so far as to suggest that "Hollywood is the global cultural capital," American media culture is a "global lingua franca," and that "America presides over a World Bank of styles and symbols, an International Cultural Fund of images and celebrities" (Gitlin 1998: 4). Sometimes the penetration of foreign culture is rather aggressive, as Ziauddin Sardar notes about people of the Third World: "…these people cannot choose what they want to be, what they have always been, because the environment that sustained and nourished them, that allowed them to be what they want to be, has been and is systematically being destroyed. They cannot live as they choose to live, because the sciences, the technologies, the medical systems, the architecture, the natural habitat that sustained their lifestyles have been suppressed and destroyed. They cannot buy what they choose to buy, because their mode of production has been replaced by imported Western consumer goods and services. They cannot even choose not to be the victims of the dominant culture: their victimisation is embedded in the global economic and political system" (Sardar 1998: 19-20).

Most modern cultures are hybrid cultures, but we shouldn't confuse hybrid culture with global culture. All artifacts and traditions finally have their own origin, and their introduction in other countries does not mean appearance of "the third global" culture. It is merely an adaptation because of some economical or political reasons. For instance, it is much cheaper for countries to purchase U.S.-produced media artifacts such as television programs than to create their own domestically. But this fact itself doesn't make U.S. television a part of global culture. It remains U.S. television, in some way adopted by local forms of culture. Mere adaptation does not make any culture or value "global." Adaptation produces hybrid culture. Global communications technologies brought us images of the horrific conflicts and inhumanity in the Persian Gulf, the former Yugoslavia, and Rwanda. These devices have made the visages of former Iraqi President Saddam Hussein, Russian President Vladimir Putin, American President George Bush and British Prime Minister Tony Blair more familiar to many Lithuanians than most of their local officials, state or even federal representatives. Personages of Anthony Burgess' *A Clockwork Orange* think and talk in the "*nadsat*" (teenage) vocabulary of the future, which is a mix of English and Russian. Modern Lithuanian teenagers use many English and Russian words in their speech, but all these facts have nothing to do with global culture. It is hybrid language representing hybrid, but not global culture and there are no nation-states' cultures that are projected globally.

Global Culture?

A third kind of culture is *global culture* itself, but, strictly speaking, there is nothing globalized in culture. Culture is concentrated identity, but identity is not in itself a barrier to openness and connectedness; to the contrary, it is a prerequisite for them. There is nothing globalized in Proust, Velásquez, Tolstoy, or Chaikovski. The more we maintain identity, the larger the scope for openness and connectedness becomes, and the more consolidated diversity becomes. In the absence of that, openness becomes capitulation, exchange becomes tutelage, and interaction becomes defeat.

The globalization of consumer technology makes it possible to transmit and receive media artifacts across geographical and cultural divides. Individuals, states, and corporations seek to consume, project, and understand these images and products, and a primary issue of the twenty-first century's global politics and social life is the power of decoding or interpreting messages and discourses of the Other. Today we have cyberspace and virtual reality, instant computerized communication all over the world; and yet have we ever felt so impoverished and isolated? And even more, not only are we impoverished but we are also aggressive in terms of modern terrorism, and violence very often means that "my truth," "my way of thinking," "my way of life" is the only way to follow for all.

Culture involves at least three components: what people think, what they do, and the material products they produce. Thus, mental processes, beliefs, knowledge, and values are parts of culture. Some anthropologists would define culture entirely as mental rules guiding behavior, although often wide divergence exists between the acknowledged rules for correct behavior and what people actually do. Consequently, some researchers pay most attention to human behavior and its material products. Culture also has several properties: it is shared, learned, symbolic, transmitted cross-generationally, adaptive, and integrated. I want to emphasize the significance of symbolic forms of transmitting for several reasons:

1. The shared aspect of culture means that it is a social phenomenon; idiosyncratic behavior is not cultural. Culture is learned, not biologically inherited, and involves arbitrarily assigned, symbolic meanings. For example, Americans are not born knowing that the color white means purity, and Lithuanians do not know that the color white means mourning in China. The human ability to assign arbitrary meaning to any object, behavior or condition makes people enormously creative and readily distinguishes culture from animal behavior. People can teach animals to respond to cultural symbols, but animals do not create their own symbols. Furthermore, animals have the capability of limited tool manufacture and use, but human tool use is extensive enough to rank as qualitatively different, and human tools always carry symbolic meanings. The symbolic element of human language, especially speech, is again a vast qualitative expansion over animal communication systems. Speech is infinitely more productive and allows people to communicate about things that are remote in time and space.

2. Culture is expressed by the external symbols that a society uses, rather than being locked inside people's heads. Clifford Geertz defines culture as "an historically transmitted pattern of meanings embodied in symbols, a system of inherited conceptions expressed in symbolic forms by means of which men communicate, perpetuate, and develop their knowledge about and their attitudes toward life" (Geertz 1973: 89). Societies use these symbols to express their "worldview, value-orientation, ethos, and other aspects of their culture (Ortner 1984: 129). Symbols are "vehicles of 'culture'" (Ortner 1984: 127), meaning that symbols should not be studied in and of themselves, but should be studied for what they can reveal to us about culture. Geertz's main point is in "how symbols shape the ways that social actors see, feel, and think about the world" (Ortner 1984: 128). Throughout his writings, Geertz has "characterized culture as a social phenomenon, as a shared system of intersubjective symbols and meanings" (Parker 1985: 62-63).

3. Culture is an active mechanism of interpretation. The knowledge of individuals is fragmented, but communicative media already have established continuity in time and space: telephone, fax, electronic mail, numerical and telematic networks, radio, television, the press, Internet, etc. Unfortunately this continuity is still not the continuity of active and living thought, singular and differentiated, emergent and cohering everywhere, but rather a network for the transportation of information. Global culture must open a new era in communication—the era of active and creative interpretation, the era of thinking together to produce new symbols for understanding of the self and the Other.

Symbols increasingly dominate international communication. Their power was demonstrated by the events of 9/11 and the war against terrorism. Yet few understand them. Now, more than ever, it is important to understand symbols in a context of global culture.

The passage to another culture does not amount to an effacement of the first but rather it is an association. Global culture exists to make this association clear, understandable, and equal. The identity is humanistically rich, and its migration takes the form of a permanent movement transcending all boundaries. Thus, language flows out of its national geographic borders, transcending them. Likewise, identity flows out of the limitations of its geographic and dynastic affiliations to become open endlessly to other identities. To make this process easy and effective there must exist a special formation with an ability to act as a universal "decoder" of traditional symbols and *Weltanschauung* of one culture into traditional symbols and *Weltanschauung* of other culture without reduction of these symbols to one fixed traditional culture.

Let us take an example: European buddhologists interpreted four traditional schools of Buddhist philosophy—*Vaibhaœhika, Sautrantika, Chittamatra,* and *Madhyamaka*—in terms of idealism vs. materialism, whereas Buddhist teaching itself had nothing to do with this purely European division. Often one symbolic system is inconsistent with another, but this inconsistency is not of an obvious character and there are many things that exist beyond the bounds of written texts or visual patterns. For each national culture, there are things that go naturally, without saying. These things do not represent themselves openly and a representative of another culture as a rule is not aware of them, and tries to understand another culture using his own cultural habits and stereotypes. As a result, we can have misunderstanding, or even a conflict. Bodily gestures and expressions, for instance, have unexpected meanings in various parts of the world. A businessman in negotiations with a Bulgarian, for example, may be surprised. The latter, in response to a query as to whether he agrees on a point, may make what seems to be an unmistakably affirmative head nod, accompanied by a soft tick of the tongue. The unknowing person cannot congratulate himself, for the gesture actually is a clear negative.

Following Durkheim, Leslie White wrote, "Human behaviour is symbolic behaviour; symbolic behaviour is human behaviour. The symbol is the universe of humanity "(White 1973: 23). Bronislaw Malinowski understood symbolism as the soul of civilization, chiefly in the form of language as a means of coordinating action or of standardizing technique, and providing rules for social, ritual, and industrial behavior (Malinowski 1992).

Cultures are based on the symbols that guide community behavior. Symbols obtain meaning from the role that they play in the patterned behavior of social life. Because of the intertwined nature of culture and traditional behavior, they cannot be studied separately. By analyzing culture, one develops a "thick description" (a term of Geertz) of a culture, which details "what the natives think they are up to." This thick description is developed by looking at both the whole culture and the parts of the culture (such as laws). "Thick description" is an interpretation of what the natives (or others) are thinking made by an outsider, who cannot think like a native.

When the world is becoming a "single place" it is of a great importance to understand the Other and to create (it would be proper to say "to rediscover") symbols that would be universal symbols. The word "universal" here doesn't mean appearance of a new culture, which is culture over all cultures. It means that these symbols pertain to the deepest level of human life regardless of nationality, local traditions, or habits. Universal symbols point to the real identity.

The situation today is that the creative movement (in literature as well as in the arts) is evolving in a way that transcends its national and linguistic ambience to assume a universal one. For between rootedness and uprootedness, between the country of birth and the country of migration, between alienation in the homeland of the self and exile in the homeland of the Other, creativity, be it "resident" or "migrant," finds expression. In its migrant aspect, in particular, it reinforces the notion of transcending an art that is imprisoned by political-national borders to assume a universal scope without detaching itself from its linguistic, civilizational, or human origins.

There always exist antinomies between universalism and particularism, between the global and the local. These issues are classic. And very often the global and universal are considered a menace to the propagation of alien culture and the destruction of originality and singularity of local cultural models. This xenophobia has a certain reason: the fear of the destruction, and the expansive and even aggressive manner of presentation of some cultural, economical, and political values. My own view is that this presentation has nothing to do with globalism and global culture. To avoid misunderstanding and unnecessary hostility it is necessary to define what is and what is not a global culture. My point is that global culture is not any particular model of culture (American, Chinese, or Russian); it is an art of interpretation, and to participate in global culture means to be able to understand artifacts of other cultures in their own contexts and to produce (by means of art, literature, or science) new knowledge codes for understanding reality and the self.

Thus, global culture has two main functions: (1) decoding, interpretation, and re-construction of existing national, local symbols with the help of anthropological, hermeneutical, and analytical studies, and (2) creating new universal symbols or knowledge codes by means of art and creative activity. These universal symbols have always existed. They are literary works of well-known authors, pictures of well-known artists, and well-known patterns of local cultures (stone gardens in Japan, native art of the people of Polynesia, traditional Russian icons, Lithuanian woodcraft, etc.). The evidence of the emergence of global culture shows itself in the appearance of a relatively new field for scientific investigations—comparative studies. To understand means to compare. To understand other cultures means to compare their values, symbols, and modes of traditional behavior with values, symbols, and modes of traditional behavior of one's native culture. Today, departments for comparative studies are almost everywhere in the world and their existence has not only academic significance. Step by step, comparativism becomes a norm for communication, particularly in multinational societies. This proves that the formation of global culture involves the art of interpretation and decoding. It is a mistake to consider comparative studies as a playground for academics; it is not a game, but a proper apparatus for mutual understanding. Perhaps it sounds strange, but it would be a good thing to create a special department for world culture and religion comparison in the UN.

Thus, global culture is not the third culture. It is the power of comparison to tie together different cultures to provide fruitful communication, understanding, and mutual rediscovery of national and local values. It is out of borders, because, as Lamartine put it: "Only selfishness and hatred have a homeland; brotherhood has no homeland."

References

Featherstone, Mike. 1995. *Undoing Culture: Globalization, Postmodernism and Identity*. London: Sage Publications.

Featherstone, Mike. 1996. *Localism, Globalism, and Cultural Identity*, in R. Wilson and N. Dissanayake (eds.), *Global/Local: Cultural Production and the Transnational Imaginary*. Durham, NC: Duke University Press.

Geertz, Clifford. 1973. "Religion as a Cultural System," in *The Interpretation of Cultures*, 87-125. New York: Basic Books, Inc.

Gellner, Ernest. 1998. *Nationalism*. New York: New York University Press.

Gitlin, Todd. "Under the Signs of Mickey Mouse and Bruce Willis." *New Perspectives Quarterly* 15 (2) (Fall 1998).

Huntington, Samuel. P. 1998. *The Clash of Civilizations and the Remaking of World Order*. New York: Touchstone Books, Simon & Schuster.

Kiley, Ray. 1998. "Introduction: Globalization, (Post-)modernity and the Third World," in Ray Kiley and Phil Marfleet (eds.), *Globalization and the Third World*. London: Routledge.

Malinowski, Bronislaw. 1992. *Magic, Science and Religion and Other Essays*. Waveland Press.

McLuhan, Marshall. 1964. *Understanding Media: The Extensions of Man*. Toronto, Ontario: The New American Library of Canada Limited.

McQuail, Dennis. 2000. *McQuail's Mass Communication Theory*, 4th ed. London: Sage Publications.

Naisbitt John. 1998. *Global Paradox: The Bigger the World Economy, the More Powerful Its Smallest Players*. New York: William Morrow & Company, Inc.

Ortner, Sherry B. "Theory in Anthropology since the Sixties." *Comparative Studies in Society and History* (1984): 129.

Parker, Richard. "From Symbolism to Interpretation: Reflections on the Work of Clifford Geertz." *Anthropology and Humanism Quarterly* 10 (3) (1985): 62-67.

Pieterse, Jan Nederveen. 1995. "Globalization as Hybridization," in Mike Featherstone, Scott Lash, and Roland Robertson (eds.), *Global Modernities*. London: Sage Publications.

Sardar, Ziauddin. 1998. *Postmodernism and the Other: The New Imperialism of Western Culture*. London: Pluto Press.

Seymour, Michel. 2000. "On Redefining the Nation," in N. Miscevic (ed), *Nationalism and Ethnic Conflict. Philosophical Perspectives*. La Salle and Chicago: Open Court.

Tehranian, Majid. 1999. *Where is the New World Order? At the End of History or a Clash of Civilizations?* in Vincent, et al. (eds.), *Towards Equity in Global Communication*, 50. Cresskill, NJ: Hampton Press, Inc.

White, Leslie. 1973. *The Concept of Culture*, 23. Burgess Intl Group.

Wiseman, John. 1998. *Global Nation? Australia and the Politics of Globalization*. Cambridge: Cambridge University Press.

Religious Plurality in Education

by Bharat Gupt

Bharat Gupt is an associate professor of English at the College of Vocational Studies, University of Delhi.

"Pluralism" is a word that these days abounds in the glib talk of undergraduates, outpourings of subaltern filmmakers, papers read by academics in international seminars, and the maiden speeches of newly elected legislators. But do we ever pause to think:

1. What exactly do we mean by the word "pluralism?"
2. What obligations and social conduct does a life of pluralism demand from its professed adherents?
3. Is pluralism a contemporary concept or have older cultures also thought of it?
4. Does the present day world have the capacity to manage variety and differences maintaining a faith in the deeper unity of humankind?

It is a pity that on this earth where plurality has been debated in metaphysical and ethical terms for thousands of years, plurality has now been debased to mean merely a tolerance of diverse faiths and cultural habits. Discussions on plurality in the context of the ultimate nature of the seen and unseen universe are no longer the order of the day. Can the diversity of dress codes, sexuality, religious convictions, and morals be practiced if the finer questions of philosophical plurality are shoved under the carpet? Reducing the larger expanse of plurality and limiting it to the sphere of "ethnic tolerance" or "community harmony" is

putting the cart before the horse. If the deeper springs of religious and social beliefs are not studied, debated, and analyzed, measures to keep the adherents of these faiths and communities in harmony are not going to succeed. Religious and cultural denominations will always be taken over by chest-beating demagogues who shall proclaim the right to dictate to their whims on behalf of vast populations. Their conflicting claims shall continue to create recurring flare-ups in the name of identity protection and continue to detract from the deeper sources of spiritual and intellectual probing.

The real worth of pluralism lies in making new and distinct choices off the beaten track. These differences created by the new choices should be profound investigations and not matters of mere practical conveniences or egotistical assertions. For example, in medieval India, the teachings of Nanak Dev, the first Guru of the Sikh denomination of Indic religions, provided a fresh method of infusing mantra repetition (*japa*) and community service in the non-iconic (*nirguna*) tradition of the devotional (*bhakti*) movement that invited adherents to his path from various religious denominations including the Muslims. Nanak chose to provide a fresh plurality and thus a new identity for spiritual uplifting and social welfare at the same time, when most of his contemporaries preached only other worldliness. But the controversies we often witness not only in India, but also in Europe and the United States, are on small matters of ethnic distinctions such as the dress codes and food habits. Thus, the insistence on the use of the turban by Sikh soldiers in the British Army or the insistence of certain Sikh organizations in India that women pillion riders on motorcycles shall not wear safety helmets cannot be taken as core issues of religious faith, as such demands are more of identity markers than spiritual practices. One could take similar examples from the Islamic and Christian folds, such as the wearing of large crosses by Christians or head scarves or skull caps that loudly declare the religious affiliations of a person more than his/her inner conduct. This show of plurality is made up of mere diversity of dress codes or marriage customs. It does not insure any deeper perceptions about the nature of reality and truth, as they are defined, for a better life according to the religious tenets of an adherent.

The obligations of societies professing pluralism go beyond mere tolerance of external markers. Such societies are obliged to cultivate actively a reasonable acquaintance with the articles of divergent faiths and beliefs. But in most national systems of formal education the world over, and particularly in the Indian one that inherits the British perspective, religious and moral education has been kept out of school and college education as a guiding principle of the secular state. For example, in the Indian educational system, it is presumed that acquainting a Muslim child with Hindu precepts will obstruct his allegiance to his family faith, and, similarly, teaching the basic tenets of Islam to a Hindu child will ruin his or her faith in tenets of parental Hinduism.

Hence, India like many a modern Western or Asian democratic non-theocratic state prefers not to teach the precepts of differ-ent religions, and especially not even of her majority religion of Hinduism to her own school children lest this kind of teaching shake the faith of the children in their parental interpretation of religion. The Indian policy makers are further afraid that if religious instruction is given, the state may be accused of promoting one religion over another, or of even pushing religious values over and above the so-called atheistic/agnostic/secular values of life that for some reason have acquired the aura of being more liberal, democratic, and modern than religious ethics. In other words, it is presumed that knowing about the faith of others, and of the majority Hindu adherents of the nation especially, is detrimental to the security and freedom of a child's beliefs.

In India, another irrational fear has been practiced for more than half a century since it was enshrined in the Constitution as an unwarranted phobia. Teaching of religion may end up as teaching of the majority religion, that is Hinduism, and this may result in a religious oppression of religious minorities like the Muslims, Christians, Buddhists, Sikhs, and atheists. Therefore, these minorities are not only "protected" by the lack of religious education, they are given a Constitutional concession to open and manage religious or other institutions where freedom to teach their particular faith is guaranteed. In other words, a minority child is likely to be harmed by exposure to the faith of the majority and, hence, receives no general religious instruction in state schools, but a majority child is not likely to be harmed if he/she attends a minority school class in a minority institution. This theory of education is based on phobia and exclusion and instills a suspicion of faiths other than one's own. Such a kinky pedagogy can only breed intolerant and ignorant members of society who can fall prey to any unhealthy cult, ranging from aggressive dogmas to terrorism promoted from within or outside the nation.

One often hears the prescription that religion and its values are best taught by the family, and the state, far from having an obligation for providing education about religious matters, should keep even the public media, such as newspapers, television, and public utility spaces sanitized from religious overtones. Besides promoting the tyranny of Euro-centric post-Enlightenment secularity, this notion simply overlooks (or secretly gloats in) the fact that the family is no longer capable of giving proper religious instruction of even the faith it professes and least of all the faiths of others. In fact, most families, even those well versed in religious concepts, have a sectarian idea and irrational emotional attachment to their faith. They teach hostility and prejudice to other faiths. It is the prejudice instilled by families that pours into the public space as strife and the more deprived the public is of education about religious matters, the greater the chances of conflict.

If plurality is to be promoted, then a new public space for religious dialogue must be created. Seminars and conventions that are now being so frantically arranged all over the world cannot resolve prejudices that families have instilled for generations. Nor is the family expected to have the pluralistic and wide-vision approach to religion that instruction in public spaces needs to evolve into a better world.

Older societies had chosen to demarcate social norms for adherents of divergent faiths in stricter terms. But people were more aware of the fundamentals of each other's religion or sect. For instance, in ancient India, a Jain child may not have gone to the same educational institution (*ashrama*) with a Buddhist or a Vaishnava child, or may never have shared lunch with a child that came from a family of the followers of Shiva, but the pedagogy of the times, as practiced in schools of all denominations, had a rigorous system of teaching the precepts of other systems, even if for the purpose of refutation. In other words, a Jain child or a mature scholar would surely know the precepts of all other sects. And so would a Buddhist or a Shaivite scholar. But what is taught nowadays in schools and universities the world over is not the way to distinguish between the why and how of different faiths, but a namby-pamby multiculturalism constantly reeling under the weight of some ideology, usually Western, be it neo-colonialism, senile socialism, or a carpetbagger globalization.

In pre-technocratic cultures, spaces of common activities were fewer than now, in the age of high mobility and intermixing. In the face of the great uniformity that occurs through mass production, perhaps religion, language, skin-color, marital laws, and food are the few markers remaining with us today for making group distinctions among vast populations. The last two, that is, marital laws and food, may not be distinct for very long and may become uniform in another half century. A hybrid global cuisine of the fast food variety and serial monogamy of the Christian heritage is already the emerging trend. Therefore, it is even more essential that an informed and open-minded view is cultivated about religion, skin-color, and language by people the world over. But in order to secure some degree of success in this direction, we must shift the emphasis from harping upon the differences among peoples, races, religions, and cultures to exploring the deeper unity of humankind.

One of the biggest hurdles in modern times regarding religious education is the distorted notion of secularity that demands a total separation of the church (not just Christian church but the organized or semimorphic body representing any religion) from the state to maintain an equal distance from all religious denominations. The events of the European Reformation and its aftermath, in which the material power of the Christian church was reduced, still hang heavy as a collective memory in social orders that inherit this civilization. This fear has made the educational systems in the West (and as much in the East where the colonial models were followed) totally divorced from religious heritage and very often valueless and hollow. And this is particularly so because the so-called Humanism of the Enlightenment has proved to be too anthropocentric and consumerist. The Marxist animosity toward religion, viewed as "opium of masses," is another major factor that contributes to the banning of religious notions from educational systems. Thus, ethics is the biggest casualty of civilization today.

It is time that the modern state should redefine its secularity to no longer mean atheism, agnosticism, or theophobia but an active engagement in imparting the basic tenets of all faiths in the world, and, specifically, those that are professed by the majority and minority populations of each land. And this should be done not as a concession but as an endeavor that answers the deepest aspirations of mankind and makes it harmonious with other beings and nonbeings on the planet. I may add here that the ideal before the Indian state, namely what has been carefully defined in India as "*sarva-dharma-sambhaava*" (equal regard for all faiths), moves in this direction. It may be noted that in the Indian philosophical systems, as in the common psyche of its people, even atheism or the Marxist materialistic dialecticism is just another faith (*matam/sampradaaya*), that is, a set of metaphysical, existential, and ethical notions that sustains its adherents. Hence, the divide between a secular and a godly system of faith does not exist, as the state is committed to the well-being of the adherents of all systems. It is then the state's duty to educate its children and adults in all the faiths so that they fulfill not only their denominational needs, but also learn to understand the faiths of others. Perhaps a rigorous pursuit of this path shall prevent us from frantically trying to dole out palliatives in emergencies, as has been the case regarding Islam after 9/11.

I, personally, have had the opportunity to be involved in some policymaking exercises regarding religious education in India. Although most of this has remained at the level of planning and is far from implementation, a fresh thinking about the content of modern education, particularly at the school level, is already underway in India. One such long exercise was conducted in 2002 at the Indira Gandhi National Center for the Arts, New Delhi, by a committee of educational experts and the then in-office chairperson of the National Women's Commission. I had the opportunity to lead the committee as the convener.

The committee and I felt that religious plurality cannot be introduced into a school curriculum as a mere verbal statement of the articles of diverse faiths to be memorized by pupils. That would be just another kind of catechism. Introducing the religious concepts should be part of the larger plan to make the young acquainted with their cultural and scientific heritage of India as a whole. Religions can make sense when they are taught in relation to architecture, dance, music, painting, poetry, drama, history and mythology, traditional medicine, and knowledge systems preserved by the forest and mountain peoples. The documented part of religious texts, the so-called scriptures, have much more meaning in relation to other forms of religious expression that depends upon music, poetry, and so many arts. As a method of collecting the advice of the schools, a series of conferences and workshops were held in which teachers and principals of about fifty schools were invited to offer their views. Much care was taken to invite teachers from Christian and Muslim schools as well as the regular schools of Hindu majority. We found that there was a great enthusiasm about changing the print-oriented and examination-modeled system of teaching and grading, and nearly all the proposals tended to demand a system in which learning would be provided through a greater involvement of the arts. It was mentioned repeatedly that the much needed communication skills could be acquired easily through various arts, and, particularly, through theater for the children.

It was emphasized that the diversified nature of Indian society as a unique mosaic of traditions and cultures, ranging from hunting-gathering communities like the primitive Jarawas of the Andaman and Nicobar Islands to the most complex urban cultures of its cosmopolitan towns, must be made familiar to students. The present school system was too centralized, elite-dominated, and urban-oriented. It will have to undergo several modifications to relate itself to the needs and conveniences of various communities and young learners if India is to have a strong base of Heritage Education (HE). The new cultural curriculum and pedagogy must take into account the life-views and living styles of the communities to which the school-going children belong and adapt the content of learning to their needs and aspirations. Severe neglect of the sense of belonging to the community makes the present-day system of schooling uninteresting and even unacceptable to many. After exhaustive discussions the following conclusions were drawn:

1. Cultural Heritage studies should be named Heritage Activity. The change in name was made to emphasize that "culture" very often stays limited to the fine arts and that students should not be asked to memorize certain facts about culture but to feel the place of culture in the broad ambience of the total heritage that includes religion, science, history, and ethics in a tangible way through practical activities to be prescribed for the classes. Culture is not an isolated activity but is a whole vision of life.

2. The Heritage Activity shall NOT be listed as extracurricular but shall be evaluated and marked as other curricular subjects. It shall be taught in all classes in the school curriculum right from primary classes through graduation.

3. Children need to be encouraged to develop more of a play-like atmosphere in tuning themselves into HA and entirely so in the lower classes through music, painting, theater, recitation, and similar arts. There should be a gradual transition from the experiential in the lower classes to the conceptual in higher classes. At all levels students shall be involved practically in learning about the material heritage (such as archaeological sites, temples, museums etc.,) and abstract heritage (philosophies, poetry, scriptures) forms of Indian Heritage through work-books, projects, and visits to sites, and less through textbooks.

4. The instructional materials of various subjects shall be divided into practical and conceptual modes of instructions, but shall be transmitted through projects and activities.

5. Besides the school system, other cultural resource centers, such as muse-

ums, historical sites, documentation centers, research institutions, places of worship holy sites, pilgrimages etc., shall be visited to foster a closeness and respect for the living heritage of the various regions of India.

6. In order to provide room for heritage activity and not impose additional workload on students, obsolete and repetitive content from the various existing subjects can be shed after proper scrutiny.

7. Training should be given to the present teachers to teach the Heritage Activity. Teachers from diverse existing subjects can very well teach HA after training. HA need not require the additional hiring of teachers.

8. Special care shall be taken to use the local, regional, and geographical aspects of Heritage around the school to accommodate the diversity of Indian culture. The HA workbooks and projects shall be prepared at state levels, but also reflect some national elements.

9. The curriculum should also be made to reflect and highlight the living urban and folk wisdom of the traditions of India.

The following themes are identified as constituting the essential aspects of India's Heritage:

a. Sacred sites and architectural heritage;

b. Folklore and lifestyles of Rural, Tribal, and Urban India;

c. Visual, Oral, Performing, and Fine Arts of India;

d. Scriptural Heritage of India, including all religious and cultural texts;

e. Literature and Literary figures of India;

f. Philosophers, Thinkers, and Saints;

g. Traditional Modes of Transmission of History, Arts, and Culture.

The creation of detailed syllabi for projects, cultural activity, workbooks, community activity, teaching of arts and crafts, etc., is a task to be undertaken by experts of various heritage subjects from early to highest class according to the suggestions and guidelines given above, should the policymakers ever decide to implement this vision of pluralism in religious and cultural education.

What has been proposed for the Indian situation above need not be treated as applicable to India alone but can be used by various countries. It is a model of treating plurality that exists in many cultures. The twentieth century has already witnessed a vast migration of Arabs and Asians into Europe, North America, and Australia. The trend is likely to intensify and to create highly diverse societies in these continents. Muslims, Sikhs, Hindus, and Orthodox Christians are now a permanent part of these regions. For this reason, the Indian conditions and the suggested model preserving harmonious diversity can be of great use to some major entities such as the United States, Canada, the United kingdom, and the European Union, which are now grappling with racial, linguistic, and ethnic conflicts. The ignorance of the Christians about Hinduism and its diverse faiths is simply appalling as one notes from the many incidents of Sikhs being mistaken as followers of Osama and shot in the United States. One may observe, though, that whereas in India much wider and intense diversity has existed for many millennia, it is relatively new in these continents and may cause more difficulties, particularly so when Christianity and Islam both preach the doctrine of the elect and the fundamental right to proselytize, which stands in the way of harmony and mutual admiration of faiths.

It is my hope that an educational policy able to open up young minds to religious diversity shall also result in locating a common ground between various religious and cultural beliefs. It may be remembered that commonality between beliefs and not their differences is the raison d'etre of communication. If communication is to be something more than exchange of goods or info-commodity, then we may benefit most from turning to the core of vibrant similarity between religions and cultural identities that exists beneath all differences and which, instead of being wiped out by individual differences, sustains itself and the differences as well. To provide a simile, it is like the consonance between two musical notes, which are always independent but are always capable of generating a mutual resonance by virtue of their common grounding in a given scale. Within our pluralism, we need to explore our common scale.

Today one cannot escape dealing with the theme of religious and cultural diversity in the context of globalization that demands harmonious interchange between cultures and nations. Hence, for a peaceful growth of global interchanges a strong mutual appreciation of religious tenets is essential. Religion happens to be one source of misunderstanding among the diverse peoples of the world, as they mostly do not understand the approaches of those who follow a faith different from theirs. This task of building understanding of different faiths cannot be left to volunteers, but should be part of the education system from childhood onward. At initial levels almost entirely, and at higher levels partially, managing the educational system is essentially the duty of the state, and governments the world over should adopt a pluralistic approach to religion in making it a part of education.

All communication rests upon an unstated presumption that differences of identities and expressions are born out of a common ground, not by themselves. In other words, the One creates the many, the Scale defines the notes. Definition of the underlying One may not be essentially theistic but can be materialistic, too, as was the case with some schools of ancient Indian philosophies such as Nyaya and Vaisheshika, and the Greek systems of philosophy such as Epicureanism and Stoicism. Identities are meaningful only so long as they interact, as do the musical notes in relation to one another. Cultures are vibrant only when they reveal their consonances. Otherwise, they stagnate or become violent, leading to self-destruction. The communicative task needs the fresh outlook of creating consonances and calls for harmony, as opposed to hegemony, which has often been the cultural agenda to create unnecessary strife.

Globalization as the Fuel of Religious and Ethnic Conflicts

by Audrey E. Kitagawa

Audrey E. Kitagawa heads an international spiritual family and is an advisor to the Office of the Special Representative of the Secretary General for Children and Armed Conflict at the United Nations. *

Economic Globalization

Economic globalization and the growth of increasingly dominant transnational corporations have accelerated at an unprecedented rate within the last twenty-five to fifty years. Modern technology has been instrumental in this acceleration, with the advent of computers, the Internet, television, transportation, and the commercialization of ideas.

Concurrently, people internationally are being affected by economic globalization, with an increasingly disproportionate distribution of wealth leaving 1.2 billion people surviving on $1 per day, and 2.8 billion people on $2 per day (U.N. Development Report). It has also led to the mass relocation of people in developing countries, who move to cities to find employment, while those in developed nations are left unemployed as companies themselves relocate to developing nations to take advantage of inexpensive labor and increased profitability.

At the end of World War II, countries strictly controlled and restricted international capital transactions while the World Bank and International Monetary Fund (IMF) facilitated international trade and investments through regulated financial flows. The relatively recent removal of these controls and restrictions has resulted in the free movement of financial capital, which is the salient feature of the globalized financial marketplace. This liberalization of international trade has created results favorable to corporate interests and wealthy nations.

Under the leadership of Ronald Reagan and Margaret Thatcher, market fundamentalism and the collapse of the Soviet Union caused the financial markets to become truly global. The erosion of controls and restrictions on financial capital and the increasing inability of countries to regulate it have opened the doorway to greater corruption, speculation, and unfair trade practices.

The Fight for Natural Resources

With the world's population doubling within the last fifty years to 6 billion people by 1999, and rising at the rate of 77 million people per year, survival and prosperity are increasingly linked to accessibility to vital resources and the potential transformation

---

* The views and opinions expressed in this article are strictly those of the author, and do not express the views or opinions of the United Nations or any other organization.

of those resources into capital flows. The population explosion and the spread of industrialization have produced an insatiable appetite for goods to accommodate the growing numbers of people.

At the end of the Cold War, strategies of containment shifted to policies of the pursuit, acquisition, and protection of essential resources as integral to security planning. The role of the military in protecting the international flow of essential materials has become crucial in the state's primary security functions.

Global demand for materials is growing at an unsustainable rate as population growth results in the consumption of more natural resources. As countries compete for the limited supply of natural resources, powerful countries are better positioned to ensure the sustainability of their own levels of consumption without regard to the impact it has on others. As the demand for these resources increases, countries where these resources are found become increasingly mired in conflict as competing interests from external as well as internal forces enter into a complex interplay of positioning for dominance and control over potential pools of wealth, as well as survival. While many of the conflicts are characterized as religious and ethnic in nature, it is the politicization of the masses through the emotionally charged fault lines of religion and ethnicity that creates the veil hiding the underlying motivation of those who drive the masses. The masses are infused with terror and fear, often subjected to heinous acts of unspeakable cruelty, pawns on an economic chessboard of power and greed.

Africa, for example, is one of the world's wealthiest continents. It has almost every resource that the world covets. It is rich in oil, minerals, gems, and timber. Huge deposits of gold, platinum, diamonds, coltan, copper, and the like are found there. Yet, the world's wealthiest continent is home to the world's poorest people, some of the world's wealthiest leaders, and some of the most prolonged and vicious conflicts.

Sub-Saharan Africa is the battlefield of two-fifths of the world's armed conflicts. More than 100 million Africans experience war daily. Sub-Saharan Africa also contains more than a third of the world's mineral reserves.

In *The Anatomy of Resource Wars*, Michel Renner (2002) details the intersections of conflict and resources, looking at the Democratic Republic of Congo, among others.

"If you purchase a cell phone…you may very well be paying to keep the war going in the Democratic Republic of Congo, where rival armies fight for control over deposits of coltan, a commodity that just over a decade ago had little commercial value, but is now vital for the one billion plus cell phones in use today. The enormous expansion of the global trade, coupled with lax or corrupt customs officials, has made access to key markets relatively easy for warring groups. Companies and rich nations that benefit from cheap raw materials have long turned a blind eye to the destruction at their source, and most consumers don't know that a number of common purchases bear the invisible imprint of violence."

As many as 2.5 million people have died since the current war in the Democratic Republic of Congo (DRC) began in 1998, and over 2 million have been displaced. More than half of them have no access to assistance. The United Nations convened a panel of experts who linked armed conflicts in the DRC with the exploitation of natural resources and foreign interests that aligned themselves with internal actors to exploit the country's resources. Trade in commodities has boomed since the war started, with the key players amassing fortunes, while millions die from malnutrition and lack the most basic goods and services.

Many of the conflicts in the DRC that occur in resource-rich areas are often reported in the media as "ethnic" conflicts, especially between the Hema and Lendu clans. What such reports often fail to include, however, is the fact that an elite network of powerful businessmen who benefit from commercial activities in the area often drive the conflict.

While governments compete with warlords, rebels, and other groups for control over resources, which earned approximately $12 billion in 2001, children, the most vulnerable of the population, suffer the most. They have been mobilized to fight in adult wars, work as laborers in mines, used as sexual slaves, and have endured a host of other abuses that have robbed them of their childhood, deprived them of their education and necessary health care, and separated them from their families and communities.

Angola, which has one of the world's poorest populations, has a large resource of diamonds. The country was stripped of approximately $4-4.2 billion in diamonds by UNITA, a rebel group that ultimately collapsed with the assassination of its leader, Jonas Savimbi. Diamonds also fueled the conflict in Sierra Leone that cut a vicious swath through the population, which saw the limbs of babies and adults alike amputated as a special signature of terror inflicted upon hapless victims.

Monies used from the sale of these resources buy weapons that arm military and paramilitary groups alike. In *Africa Betrayed*, George B. N. Ayittey (1991: 153) writes, "Military spending by African countries, according to the U.S. Center for Defense Information, reached $16.9 billion in 1983, up 400 percent from $3.8 billion in 1973. Sixteen African countries spent more on arms than they received in aid…. Angola, hard hit by drought, spent $525 million on arms, and received $502 million in aid. Nigeria and Mozambique spent $430 million and $260 million, respectively, on arms, and received $48 million and $242 million, respectively, in aid."

The Case of Nigeria

Nigeria is a country rich in petroleum. Multinational oil companies have exploited this country to the detriment of the people, who have been relegated to poverty and have endured the destruction of their environment, especially in the Niger Delta region, which is rich in oil. Anup Shah (2000), in his article, "Conflict in Africa," citing part of the conclusion of a report, "Oil for Nothing: Multinational Corporations, Environmental Destruction, Death and Impunity in the Niger Delta" notes:

While the story told to consumers of Nigerian crude in the United States and the European Union via ad campaigns and other public relations efforts…is that oil companies are a positive force in Nigeria, providing much needed economic development resources, the reality that confronted our delegation was quite the opposite. Our delegates observed almost every large multinational oil company operating in the Niger Delta employing inadequate environmental standards, public health standards, human rights standards, and relations with affected communities. These corporations' acts of charity are slaps in the face of those they claim to be helping. Far from being a positive force, these oil companies act as a destabilizing force, pitting one community against another, and acting as a catalyst…together with the military with whom they work closely…to some of the violence racking the region today.

The impact of the multinational oil operations in the Niger Delta area is central to community protests and conflicts, with the companies often favoring one local community over another, provoking rivalries. The inability of the people to derive benefits from the wealth of oil resources and economic inequalities, rather than ideological and communal differences, results in violence. The characterization of these clashes as "tribal" or "ethnic" creates a negative stereotype of a people's failure to get along, and belies the underlying causes, which point to the social and economic marginalization and degradation of the people.

Nigeria has suffered from religious clashes between Muslims and Christians. The population is approximately 50 percent Muslim, 40 percent Christian, and 10 percent "traditionalists." In its early days of independence, religion was not an issue in mainstream politics even though conflicts between and within regions were severe. Religion was made an issue through the successive militarization of politics and the coups, counter coups, and assassinations of leaders of one faith by those of another faith.

For example, in January 1966, Ahmadu Bello, Muslim premier of the Northern Region was assassinated by Major General Johnson T.U. Ironsi, a Christian Igbo. Bello was part of the first civilian and democratic government that was overthrown in a violent coup. Ironsi led a military government, and suspended regional and national constitutions. The north reacted violently, and in July 1966, Ironsi was killed in a coup led by Muslim Hausa officers.

Ironsi was succeeded by another Christian, Lt. Colonel Yakubu Gowan, who headed a military government, and was eventually overthrown by General Murtala Ramat Mohammed, a Northern Muslim. The Christians accused Mohammed of an agenda to Islamize the country. In a bloody coup d'etat, Lt. General Olusegun Obasanjo, a Christian, was appointed head of state and commander in chief of the armed forces. After three years, Obasanjo turned over the country to civilian Alhaji Shegu Shagari for a return to civilian rule. However, Muslim Mohammed Buhari ousted Shagari after having held office for almost four years, and named himself head of the Supreme Military Council, and remilitarized politics.

Two years later, he was replaced by Major General Ibrahim Babangida, a Muslim, who promised a return to civilian rule. During his eight years as a military dictator, the country experienced its greatest frequency of religious conflicts. Babangida played the Muslims against the Christians, and kept the populace distracted with religious conflict as a way to divert attention away from the real problems confronting them. After eight years in office, Babangida stepped down, and was succeeded by civilian Ernest Shonekan, who, within three months, was replaced in a coup by General Sani Abacha, a Muslim, who became the next military dictator for the next five years until his sudden death from a heart attack. His successor, General Abdulsalami Abubakar, a Muslim, promised to return the country to a democratically elected government. After one year, Abubakar stepped down, and Obasanjo took over as the first democratically elected president, ending a nearly thirty-year military rule by Northern Muslims.

Central to the politics of dominance was the political, social, and economic privileges and patronage controlled by the group in power. Religious and ethnic differences were used as justification for conflict, but in reality, they were tools of manipulation to marginalize the have-nots and protect the needs and interests of the haves. Unfortunately, those in power were corrupt, and diverted billions of dollars of oil revenue and public funds into their private bank accounts.

During Nigeria's oil boom of the 1970s wealth was easy to obtain by those who were well placed. Favorable market conditions yielded oil revenues of $39 billion per year. Government contracts, kickbacks, purchases, and loans were all managed to divert funds into the hands of the elite and politically well connected. In 1986, a government investigation estimated that approximately $25 million a day was being transferred abroad at the height of the oil boom in 1978.

Simultaneously, Nigeria incurred a $32 billion foreign debt while $33 billion was held by Nigerians in foreign bank accounts. Corruption permeated the public sector. The power elites shamelessly dipped their hands into the public coffers and treated it as their own private funds. This crippled Nigeria's economy and fueled turmoil and conflict between the different religious and ethnic groups.

Even though Nigeria returned to civilian rule in 1999, the impact of globalization has fostered years of corruption, the politicization of religion and ethnicity, the rise of militarism, and the growing disparity between the rich and the poor. Since 1999, approximately 10,000 people have died in regional, ethnic, and religious fighting, and the people continue to live in the throes of violence and poverty (Project Ploughshares 2003).

The Need for Reform

Financial markets are amoral, and allow people and companies to act in their own interests. Financial markets are designed to create wealth and the accumulation of profit. They are not designed to take care of social needs. Markets deal with the exchange of goods and services and do not deal with issues of morality and social justice. Historically, the realm of legislating morality has been left to the arena of politics and states. When these arenas themselves, however, become the tools that enable and perpetrate some of the worst human rights violations, environmental degradation, corruption, and expenditures of obscene sums on the machineries and mechanisms of war, which lead to the polarization of the masses in destructive ways, economic globalization as it exists in its current state is in need of reform.

There must be greater transparency on the inner workings of the international financial institutions, and changes to their organizational structures of governance and accountability, as well as to their policies and practices. These policies have favored transnational corporations and wealthy countries, and created tremendous debts for developing countries, often compelling these countries to adopt policies and practices that have not always served them well.

The lack of transparency of the International Monetary Fund and the World Bank makes it difficult for anyone not privy to the inner workings of the institutions to find or interpret many of the documents produced, or to know what decisions are being made, and by whom. There is a significant lack of information about the activities of the executive boards. Decisions are taken by consensus, and information is not released as to who supported or opposed decisions taken.

Formal voting power is determined by a formula weighted to economic strength with developed countries accounting for 61 and 62 percent of voting strength in the

World Bank and IMF, respectively. The United States also has the power of block voting over the principle decisions of these institutions. This structure works to the detriment of developing countries because the developed countries have the power to promote policies and practices that serve their own interests.

Joseph Stiglitz (2003:18), former chief economist and senior vice president of the World Bank wrote:

...the policies of the international economic institutions are all too often closely aligned with the commercial and financial interests of those in the advanced industrial countries...the Washington Consensus has all too often been to benefit the few at the expense of the many, the well-off at the expense of the poor. In many cases commercial interests and values have superseded concern for the environment, democracy, human rights and social justice.

The Washington Consensus promoted market fundamentalism, which was, in turn, imposed without adequate consideration of the stage of political and economic structures and development of the country. This, in turn, opened the doorway to instability and economic crises.

The changing missions and roles of the IMF and the World Bank also led to duplicative actions and conflicting functions. The ultimate result has been a decrease in the effectiveness of the institutions, and an exacerbation of the difficulties that they are supposed to remedy. In the beginning, the mission of the IMF was to maintain stability for monetary exchange rates, and the World Bank was to provide capital to help rebuild Europe, and spur development in less developed countries.

With the demise of the system of fixed exchange rates, the IMF sought a new purpose. It began to move into development and structural adjustment lending, and began to expand in a careless way. The World Bank began to move into economic policy and developmental areas such as environment and labor. The changes in the roles and missions of the institutions brought them into conflict with each other wherever their policy recommendations diverged. The financial crises in Asia, Russia, Argentina, and Brazil indicate that the international financial institutions, now far from their original missions, could not adequately deal with the challenges of the modern economy.

While market fundamentalism abhors regulation, banking regulations in developing and developed countries need to be improved. Sound banking systems are crucial to stability. Further, the debt of developing countries should be written off. IMF and World Bank loans and credits are key components of the massive debt burdens of developing countries. The IMF should return to the spirit of its original mission by restricting lending to short-term liquidity, and ending its current practice of extending long-term loans. The World Bank should likewise restrict its loans and grants to the poorest of the developing countries that do not have access to private markets, and curb the majority of its loans that now go to middle-income developing countries that have abundant access to private markets.

The international financial institutions should further exercise greater responsibility in loaning money to countries plagued with corruption and governments that fail to account for the funds received. Much of the money provided to governments with high levels of corruption do not go to help the countries' poor people, but have served to enrich the corrupt leaders who wasted, squandered, or stole the funds for their own enrichment.

The World Trade Organization needs a more balanced trade agenda. Developed countries have succeeded in opening the markets of the developing countries to their products, while restricting and closing their markets to the products of the developing countries. Developed countries' heavily subsidized farmers and industries make it impossible for developing countries to compete. Because of the unfair trade agenda, the poorer countries have not received their fair share of benefits. In fact, Sub-Sahara Africa has suffered greater decline because of current trade practices and policies, and the constant conflicts that have arisen over its vast reserves of mineral deposits.

Governments must take responsibility for implementing governmental transparency and accountability to stem corruption and abuse, and be willing to take decisions that will best serve their people.

Governments and business enterprises must adhere to international human rights and humanitarian and environmental standards. While voluntary initiatives for businesses serve as useful guidelines, they lack the power of enforcement, accountability, and monitoring mechanisms.

Finally, the ultimate consumers of these resources must also be willing to reform their daily habits, consumption patterns, and purchasing choices to stem the bloodletting and misery that their voracious and indiscriminate appetites create.

Conclusion

Economic globalization has brought benefits and disadvantages. It has enlivened societies to work at retaining their unique cultural, religious, and ethnic identities as markets increasingly bring uniformity and sameness everywhere. It has simultaneously sharpened cultural, religious, and ethnic differences as groups compete for resources, accessibility to goods, services, jobs, and a host of other necessities. It has also polarized groups toward heightened conflict and violence as they become increasingly politicized and manipulated by complex internal and external forces that seek greater consolidation of power and wealth into fewer hands.

As we study ways in which institutional, governmental, business, and individual reforms must take place, we must also work together to develop and cultivate cultures of peace and dialogue. Each person must feel it to be his/her duty to live by those values, ethics, and principles that speak for compassion, caring, and respect for others. To step into the shoes of global citizenship means that we must not abdicate our responsibilities to be aware of what is on the global landscape that adversely impacts our fellow human beings. It also means that we must be willing to actively undertake those steps that will redress those adversities.

We live in an interconnected world, and the degradation of one human being is the degradation of us all. Wherever human rights abuses occur, wherever humanitarian relief is needed, wherever human suffering exists we must not turn a blind eye. We should tell the stories of truth that we may learn the ways of truth, and grow in the wisdom of humility, which would turn the suffering that arrogance, greed, and self interest have wrought into lessons of equity and justice.

References

Ayittey, George B. N. 1991. *Africa Betrayed.* New York: St. Martin's Press.

Chua, Amy. 2003. *World on Fire.* New York: Doubleday.

Klare, Michael T. 2001. *Resource Wars: The New Landscape of Global Conflict.* New York: Metropolitan Books, Henry Holt.

Kretzmann, Steve. 2003. "Oil, Security, War: The Geopolitics of US Energy Planning." *Multinational Monitor* 24 (1/2).

Machel, Graca. 2001. *The Impact of War on Children.* New York: Palgrave.

Maier, Karl. 2000. *This House Has Fallen.* Cambridge, MA: Westview Press.

Mofid, Kamran. 2002. *Globalization for the Common Good.* London: Shepheard-Walwyn Ltd.

Project Ploughshares. 2003. *Armed Conflicts Report.* Online. Available at: http://www.ploughshares.ca/CONTENT/ACR/ACR00/ACR00.html.

Renner, Michael. 2002. The Anatomy of Resource Wars. Worldwatch paper #162. Available at: http://www.worldwatch.org

Schwab, Peter. 2001. *Africa, a Continent Self Destructs.* New York: Palgrave Press.

Shah, Anup. 2000. *Nigeria and Oil.* Global Issues. Online. Available at: http://www.globalissues.org/Geopolitics/Africa/Nigeria.asp.

Soros, George. 2002. *George Soros on Globalization.* New York: PublicAffairs.

Stiglitz, Joseph E. 2003. *Globalization and Its Discontents.* New York: W.W. Norton & Co. United Nations Development Programme. 2001. *UN Human Development Report.* New York: Oxford University Press.

United Nations Development Programme. 2003. *UN Human Development Report.* New York: Oxford University Press.

United Nations Panel of Experts on the Illegal Exploitation of Natural Resources and Other Forms of Wealth of the Democratic Republic of Congo. 2002. *Final Report of the Panel of Experts on the Illegal Exploitation of Natural Resources and Other Forms of Wealth of the Democratic Republic of Congo.* Accessed online at: http://www.natural-resources.org/minerals/CD/docs/other/565e.pdf.

Turmoil in Babel

by Adelani F. Ogunrinade

Adelani F. Ogunrinade is a professor and director of the Graduate Studies and Research at the University of Technology, Jamaica.

Introduction

Globalization, defined in terms of integration of local economies into the global market, is not a new phenomenon in Africa. As Thornton (1998) pointed out, commerce with Europe by Africa dates back to around 1400, through exchange of raw materials (mainly gold) and slave labor for finished goods (cloth, iron, and munitions). The actual motivation for European trade with Africa was not the product of "a long range visionary scheme or an explosion of commerce or even the response to new technology, it was little more than an opportunity to gain immediate profits through seizure or purchase of goods by using existing technology and small amounts of capital." This was later reinforced by the growth of the great trading companies under charter from European countries. This period ended by the mid- to late twentieth century. This period represented the defining moment for the alignment of Africa's commerce with European markets and paved the way for Africa's integration with the global economy. Walter Rodney (quoted by Thorton, 1998) described this as the "first decisive step towards the marginalization of Africa through the creation of an economic dependency."

Globalization defined in terms of increasing universalization of capitalism, the integration of local economies into the global economy, the promotion of information technology, and the establishment of political institutions of the Western democratic ideal, has a "celebratory" character to it. Touted as the panacea to all the economic woes of Africa-openness to trade, free flows of capital, goods, and ideas, especially through the medium of new powerful information technologies, are said to promote economic growth for developing economies, allowing them to reap the economies of scale thereby boosting export earnings and bringing them "Mammon's plums." As Nicholas Stern, vice president of the World Bank pointed out, the economic impact of globalization has led to successful integration of local markets and poverty reduction in a number of countries. Some poor countries, which twenty years ago were exporters of primary commodities (e.g., Bangladesh, Vietnam, India), now venture into the manufacturing and services industry. This has led to wide-scale poverty reduction and their inclusion into the global economy. Indeed, capital flows of foreign direct investment to developing countries, which amounted to $160 billion in 1991, had increased to $1.4 trillion by 2000. Nevertheless, there are also losers in globalization and those who have been marginalized through its unevenness and power asymmetry. These are the subordinates of trade and capitalism! For instance, economic growth in Sub-Saharan African remained stagnant in 2003 because of its dependence on European growth, which contracted to 0.7 percent in 2003.

Furthermore, there are "invisible borders" against "free trade," militating against developing countries and preventing them from gaining full access to the gains of globalization (Asobie 2001; Gibbon 2002; Goff 2001). Worse still, the new international trade regime that emerged after the Uruguay Round in 1994 has exposed the twin tendencies of encouraging increased participation of African countries in some sectors of global trade while simultaneously discouraging participation by raising global barriers to free trade through imposition of stiff market entry conditions and mandatory global norms (Gibbon 2002; Diamond 2002). Consequently, powerful economies and transnational corporations are the major beneficiaries of global flows of capital. In 1989, the countries with 20 percent of the richest world's population received 82.7 percent of total global income, while countries with the poorest 20 percent received 1.4 percent, a ratio of 59:1. As President Mbeki of South Africa aptly captures it, "there are two global villages—one getting richer and the other getting poorer."

Social transformation theory as a new analytical framework, posits that development can no longer be defined only in terms of economic indices and that globalization has far-reaching social consequences which may constitute new forms of destabilization, undermining the ability of nation states to control their economic destiny, social policies, and culture (Castles 2001). The cultural impact of such "distanciated" relations and the dialectics of local-global relationships as manifested not only in terms of a new global culture of dressing, eating, language, and music have been extensively reviewed in Tomlinson (1999). The transformative effects of globalization have been described in terms of homogenization, "cultural dis-embedding," "de-territorialization," hybridization, and "transculturalism," but there are counter-arguments against what appears on the surface to be trappings of a "monoculture of global capitalist imperialism." The latter has been described as the "fallacy of internationalism" since culture may be much more robust than is imagined. However, as pointed out by Tomlinson (1999), the impact of globalization goes further than these aspects of "mundane cosmopolitanism" and its many disguises, to involve the deepening complex network and interdependencies that characterize the globalized world.

The process of globalization and its effects on nation states will be reviewed here through an analysis of postcolonial legacies in Nigeria. The questions are: How has globalization impacted Nigeria's cultural diversity and in what forms do societies respond to globalization? I seek to identify the various social challenges to nationhood as a result of the global economic environment and the activities of transnational corporations. How have diverse groups in Nigeria, in turn, responded to the globalizing forces? I examine some solutions for the stabilization of Nigerian democracy in order to harness the gains of globalization.

Why Nigeria?

Nigeria is a good case study for the unfolding drama of the impact of globalization on a developing economy. First, Nigeria is a capitalist state without the usual trappings of a well-ordered capitalist economy, or, what Achebe (1987) calls a "second-class, hand-me-down capitalism." Secondly, there is the sheer size of the local market, the large population

(120 million) and the political and economic dominance of Nigeria in African affairs. A modern day "tower of Babel," Nigeria has about 250 ethnic groups speaking over 450 tongues and dialects. Nigeria's peoples are almost evenly divided between Muslims and Christians, with many in both faiths resorting to traditional divinity, especially during times of adversity. The introduction of Islam into Northern Nigeria because of the trans-Saharan trade and the Fulani jihad of Uthman Dan Fodio meant that a substantial portion of Northern Nigeria was ruled through emirs who owed allegiance to the Sultan. On the other hand, because of its access to the sea, Southern Nigeria had a preponderance of Western education and Christianity acquired through the influence of the Christian missionaries. There is also the cultural dualism: a clash of cultures, values, and political systems in indigenous peoples that arose through the erosion of traditional values following the colonial influence, resulting in a weakness of the traditional checks and balances of power. Colonialism resulted in a "passive participant" rather than "responsive participant" system of democracy. It created two realms of political thought on the citizen—the communal realm of ethnic and sub-ethnic allegiances, and a universal civic realm in which citizenship was universal. British colonialism also introduced direct rule in Southern Nigeria, where Western education and Christianity were in place, and a system of indirect rule through the emirs and traditional rulers in the North, thereby producing conflicting signals of democracy in the South and feudalism in Northern Nigeria (IDEA 2002). The net effect was that Nigeria at independence was a hotchpotch contraption of several nationalities. Chief Awolowo had described Nigeria then not as "a nation but a mere geographical expression"

Postcolonial Legacies and Nigeria's Economic Crisis

The dominance of commodity trade has shaped most of the economy of post-independence Africa. Nigeria's primary export was cocoa from the western region of Nigeria, palm oil from the east and groundnuts and cotton from the northern parts of the country. In her book, *Economic Reforms and Nigeria's Political Crisis*, Umoren (2001) chronicled the events leading to Nigeria's economic crisis. In the first decade of independence, Nigeria remained a conventional commodity-based economy following the decline in oil, with agricultural produce accounting for 80 percent of exports. From 1971, petroleum gradually became the main stay of the economy, accounting for about 89 percent of the total government revenues and 98 percent of its foreign exchange earnings. The fluctuations of commodity prices and Nigeria's over-dependence on oil as agricultural produce declined, deteriorated the economy during early 1980s. Prior to 1970, Nigeria was a cautious borrower on the world market, shopping mainly for short-term or medium-term loans, sometimes at concessionary rates. However, by 1976, Nigeria had thrown caution to the wind following a temporary surge in oil prices, and the young and often immature military leaders had begun to brag that money was not Nigeria's problem. Nigeria went into big-time spending and even bigger-time borrowing. All manner of creditors and "economic hitman" were in competition to lend with equal vigor. Undoubtedly, some of the money found its way back to the bank vaults of the lending nations through corruption, kickbacks, and contract scams. The bookkeeping of the debts was badly carried out. Some of the debts are still not reconcilable, and may even be phantom debts without any documentation.

In 1978, Nigeria negotiated a Euromarket loan of $1 billion dollars—the biggest ever obtained by an African country. By 1984, the management of the debt portfolio had deteriorated so badly that no one even paid attention to the size of the debt. With Nigeria's perceived oil wealth, the credit line was kept open. More borrowing followed until the signs of distress began to show. By 1986 external debt, which amounted to just 186.9 percent of export earnings, had grown large because of unmet debt service commitments, and it had become obvious that Nigeria had to adjust its economy either through a monetary or structural mechanism. By June of 1986, Nigeria agreed with the International Monetary Fund (IMF) to devalue its currency and liberalize trade, structural factors that led to the failure of Structural Adjustment Program (SAP). The World Bank developed only a "one size fits all" model for African countries. World Bank policy with respect to SAP did not differentiate between "a good project in a poor country and a bad project in a rich country." The design of various projects did not benefit from empirical analysis as it was a learning- by- doing approach. By the end of 1982, Nigeria's external debt service had grown to $134 million or 4.9 percent of GNP while the total debt portfolio was $13.5 billion. Over the period, Nigeria has paid over $43 billion U.S. in interest charges alone to service a debt of 13.5 billion!

The rising cost of capital, due to high interest rates and the declining purchasing power, led to a reduction in capacity utilization of industries. Furthermore, the dwindling revenue base, due to the collapse of oil prices, resulted in a failure of the second objective of achieving fiscal balance.

Inflation remained high, far ahead of growth and there was unprecedented devaluation of the Naira vis-à-vis the U.S. dollar. This inflationary spiral was due to the removal of subsidies, an unstable foreign exchange market, privatization and commercialization, and the fiscal deficit. To make matters worse, the overall efficiency of the public sector remained poor.

The debt also discouraged domestic and foreign investment. The socioeconomic impact of the structural adjustments and debt peonage started to be felt in Nigeria by 1990 (Banjura 1989) .The purchasing power declined as per capita income dwindled from $610 in 1986 to $290 in 1990. The unemployment rate increased from a composite 5.3 percent in 1986 and the labor sector profile began to change as more rural urban drift continued to be felt. Food prices soared by 28 percent and negative effects began to be felt on health, nutrition, education, and the environment. On education, UNECA stated that "the reduction in public expenditures on education in absolute and relative terms necessitated by stabilization and structural adjustment programs resulted in a reversal of the earlier trends of the 1960s, and this had potential consequences for social transformation."

Social Impact of the New Global Market Regime

Globalization has subjected the traditional functions of family, community, and nation-state in Africa to all forms of pressures, most of which arose from the debt overhang, reduced FDI, and the deleterious effect of uneven trade liberalization on social provisioning. Thirty-three out of the forty-five heavily indebted poor countries are from Sub-Saharan Africa, and servicing this debt has been quite exacting in terms of provisioning for infrastructure and social services (Aaron 2001). There is the social cost of debt peonage, which amounted to about $187 billion in thirty African countries between 1970 and 1996. Although world foreign direct investment was $245.3 billion between 1991 and 1996, Africa's FDI was a mere $4.5 billion or 1.5 percent. Several African countries are involved in civil wars and sporadic outbursts of violence due to attempts to buoy their foreign exchange earnings through illegal trade in "conflict minerals." Besides, public sector rationalization and privatization has led to a reduction in patronage and less flexibility in dealing with political crises. Decentralization of power has led to more opening up of rural areas to political activities. Inflation and privatization has led to an army of unemployed young men, and this has resulted in an ever-rising crime wave and social upheavals (Tomlinson 1999).

Preventable death due to malaria and diarrheal disease took a toll on infants, women, and the elderly due to inadequate funding of public health facilities, high costs of drugs, and the reduction in ability of rural residents to purchase imported drugs. Reduction in time and space through travel may have aided the spread of HIV/AIDS throughout Africa and the rest of the world. The negative effects of globalization on food security have already been discussed by Kent (1999). Pricing patterns favor the rich. Poor countries are forced to bear a disproportionate share of risks. The final touch is the digital divide and its implications for poor countries. As high technology becomes increasingly important, poorer countries with fewer resources and less educated workforces will be left behind. Ironically, the technologi-

cal divide and capital flows have continued to fuel a brain drain from the South to the North.

Globalization, Nationalism, and Ethnicity

One of the paradoxes of the advance of globalization is that it has led to all forms of particularization and a reversion to ethnicity (Davidson 1992). In Nigeria, this has been manifest through the accentuation of ethnic and religious cleavages within the country (IDEA 2002; Mamdani 1998; Salih 2000). Although some of these tensions may be traced to ancestral ethnic and linguistic cleavages, the tension between haves and have-nots in terms of the produce of capitalism may have continued to fuel the conflict. For instance, the incessant crises in Kano (Northern Nigeria) between the predominantly Muslim (Northern) Hausa and the more prosperous and more educated Christian trader-settlers in Kano may have this basis.

Although political violence is not new in Nigeria's postcolonial history, a more perplexing issue is the sporadic violence that has characterized democratic rule in Nigeria since 1999. Since that time, Nigeria has witnessed a spiral of ethnic and religious conflicts, which has led to about 10,000 deaths within the last three years—coinciding with the period of the new democratic dispensation. There has been the emergence and coalition of political and ethnic forces in such groups as the *Afenifere*—a pan-Yoruba group (first established as *Egbe Omo Oduduwa* in 1948 by Yoruba students in the UK). The group is now being resuscitated into the political unit known as Alliance for Democracy (AD)—as the dominant party in Western Nigeria following the 1999 elections. The *Arewa Consul-*

tative Forum in the North, which is the replacement for the hitherto shadowy "Kaduna mafia," is a group of Northern elites sworn to protecting the political interest of the North and *Ohaneze* as the Igbo umbrella group in Eastern Nigeria (an offshoot of the Igbo National Union of the 1940s). All these groups complete with their militias—the *Oodua* Peoples Congress (OPC) in the West, the *Bakassi* and *Egbesu* boys in the East, and the Arewa Peoples Congress (APC) in the North—operate as alternative security outfits with impunity. Despite their legal proscription by the federal government, these political groupings have survived. What is even more surprising is the membership of the ethnic groups, which cuts across age, gender, and profession, involving former Nigerian heads of state and otherwise leading proponents of the Nigerian project. These groups, including the professional associations (journalists, bar, medical, etc.) continue to provide a vehicle for the divisive pressures of Nigeria's cultural pluralism and have led to increasing demands for the restructuring of the Nigerian state through a "sovereign national conference." In response to the demand for political restructuring, the federal government of Nigeria side-stepped the constitutionally elected representatives in the National Assembly and instituted its own National dialogue. In February 2005, the federal government handpicked "elder statesmen" and other representatives of diverse groups to achieve its aim. However, opposition groups (the PRONACO) have threatened to call their own alternative conference to look at the whole issue of Nigeria's peaceful coexistence among different nationalities.

In the Niger delta, wide-scale riots between Itsekiri and the Urhobo over land rights, and wrangles over compensation from oil companies have kept the oil city of Warri on the boil. While the transnational oil companies have tried to respond to charges of neglect and environmental degradation through funding community projects, it is not in doubt that they took active interest in arming the local police and pacifying the areas of their operation by providing arms and logistics to the local police (Mamdani 1998). Violent takeovers of oil rigs and the kidnapping of oil workers by restless youths for ransom money added a new dimension to the struggle for mineral rights popularized by the Ogoni struggle, led by the late Ken Sao-Wiwa (who was brutally murdered by the military regime of General Abacha). Similar pressures may be at play in today's Saudi Arabia, which pitches the pro-American ruling class against the more restless Islamic fundamentalists of the Al Qaeda sect.

Abubakar believes that large-scale movement of people, resulting from a modern world economy, has constantly undermined ethno-linguistic homogeneity and led to tensions and conflicts. Here we encounter localization at the expense of globalization—a rebirth of ethnic irredentism, regionalism, and factionalism, a sort of "*China Town*" complex or what Dijkstra et al. (2001) call the "precarious balance between global flows and cultural closure—the culturally homogenizing and the simultaneously heterogenizing opposite effect of globalization." We have already noted the manipulation of these ethnic political groups for elite advantage in Nigeria. However, Dijkstra et al.(2001) have explained the dual process of globalization and localization (which he termed "glocalisation") as constantly feeding on each other. People's awareness of being involved in open-ended global flows seem to trigger a search for a fixed orientation. The three elements of territory, people, and culture combine to form the country but people belong to one culture. The continuous forging of cultural identity in the crucible of the historical struggle for land and resources among "sons of the soil" (indigenes) and settlers, makes the ethnic identity stronger than the civic or global identity. As Mamdani (1998) explains, the sense of the ethnic can be far more important than the civic, especially to the poor in Africa because ethnic identity is the only way for the poor to gain access to land.

The notion that the Nigerian crisis is an inter-ethnic conflict rather than an intra-elite conflict has been contested. In a profound analysis of the origins of elite conflict, Joseph et al. (1996) argue that colonial policy created an elite group of educated civil servants, most of them of southern Nigeria origin, in order to stabilize the colonial enterprise and the interventionist state. However, the new elite soon learned the tricks of the trade built on the exploitative logic of the colonial enterprise. The emerging anti-colonial movement used its position to pursue personal and ethnic interest from a perspective that all moral and material advantages depended on who holds power and that the end justified the means.

Shifts in Labor Migration Patterns

A consequence of the capital flows caused by globalization is the shift in labor migration patterns. This was first observed in the form of rural/urban migration in the 1980s and later in the intellectual capital flight (the brain drain), which involved major movements of Nigerian professionals in search of foreign-exchange and higher wages. It is estimated that about 100,000 Nigerian doctors and other professionals live and work in the United States while a whole range of other migrant Nigerian professionals are visible in South Africa, UK, and indeed, all parts of the world. An estimated 20,000 Nigerian sex workers ply their trade in Italy and other European countries. Those Nigerians who have not been able to market their skills by legitimate means have resorted to illegitimate means through crime syndicates, such as the "Advanced fee fraud-419," electronic credit card scams, and drug trafficking. The new information age has unleashed these new electronic crimes on a global scale through the transnational networks of the Internet and other electronic media (faxes, emails, etc). In the amoral world of capitalism, which exists in Nigeria, these crimes have sometimes been justified as some form of "reparation" or "debt forgiveness." However, they were crimes relatively unknown to Nigerians before the advent of the new global economic regime of the early 1980s.

Globalization and Corruption

There is hardly anything written about Nigeria without the issue of corruption being mentioned. In terms of the Corruption Perception Index released by Transparency International, Nigeria ranks third, scoring 1.6 behind Haiti and Bangladesh (1.5). News about Nigeria's late politico, General Sani Abacha, siphoning up to 4 billion U.S. dollars from the state coffers into Swiss, British, and American bank accounts is particularly galling. Ironically, the fact that Western banks and financial institutions provide safe off-shore havens for such looted funds indicates that they are also active participants in the corruption network and money laundering for Third-World despots. However, corruption and greed are universal attributes of all societies—first or Third World as the

Enrons, Worldcoms, and the Martha Stewarts attest. Some writers have even argued that "greed works," either at the corporate or the individual level. They suggest that greed inspires the capitalist dreams of increasing productivity.

In pre-colonial Africa, political corruption and bribery were not entirely reprehensible, as they were seen as traditional forms of paying obeisance to rulers who were ordained by the gods to rule. Only when the rulers were too greedy or too tyrannical were they subject to sanctions. The word *kola or kolanut gift* in Nigerian parlance is one form of paying homage to the rulers. In colonial times, elite greed replaced this form of traditional obeisance and kola became a euphemism for bribery—and an illegal exchange of formal and informal services between the ruling elite and the ruled. Since colonialism was an imposition, political corruption became justified as a form of disobedience to the crown—through evasion of taxes, withholding of revenue, etc. However, these acts of illegality soon became a network of illegal transactions and exploitation. You paid to bribe the grossly underpaid police or the sanitary inspector some kola in order to avoid arrest (even for trumped-up charges) and they, in turn, bribed the school principal for admission of their children. Neither the police nor the school principal had to declare kola; it worked for the lawbreaker and the enforcer, neither of which had any particular stake in the colonial enterprise. Since post-independent states were also the creation of the colonial enterprise, there was no particular loyalty to the new nation either, and the whole process became well-oiled, especially as incomes dwindled following the fall of commodity prices and the biting debt peonage. Political corruption then began to be seen as a share of the national cake. It formed the basis of the so-called "prebendalism" during which local representatives go to take their own share of the cake from the national pot, to the acclaim of their kith and kin.

Diamond (2002) has contrasted civil society built on trust and respect for law against such a predatory network, which, in the case of Nigeria was reinforced by many years of governance under a cynical and plundering military class. "The masses of ordinary people at the bottom of a predatory society," argues Diamond, "cannot cooperate because they are trapped in hierarchical networks of corruption." The policeman takes a bribe from the school principal who, in turn, takes a bribe to admit the son of the policeman to school. The network is reinforced by ethnic, religious, and identity cleavages that keep the oppressed from collaborating. Government then becomes (not a public enterprise, but a criminal conspiracy and an organized crime). Global networks of electronic and information technology, travel, and information flows have now reinforced local corruption so that it becomes easier for a local governor to transfer money from state coffers into a London account on the same day. It is an open secret that many multinational corporations actively bribe or "lobby" local politicians in order to obtain lucrative contracts, sometimes paying 10-50 percent of upwardly revised contracts into the pockets of politicians through "mobilization fees."

Globalization, Ethnicity, and the New Information Order

Nigeria has about twenty daily newspapers, about thirty weekly magazines, and up to forty TV stations, the majority owned mostly by private entrepreneurs from Southern Nigeria (the so-called Lagos—

Ibadan axis). The geographically skewed ownership has tended to polarize public opinion along the divisions of the old North and South. Anderson (1983) describes the nation as an "imagined community" where loyalty to each other and the country occurs through print capitalism. Other theorists have recognized the contributions of the culture industry to meaning making and identity formation, fostered especially through the mediation of the audiovisual industry (Gibbon 2002). Witness the "rastafarization" of the black world through Bob Marley's reggae music and hairstyle.

This instantaneous effect of the culture industry was felt during the *Miss World* riots in 2002 when a Southern-Nigerian-based Christian journalist, Miss Chioma Daniel, wrote that Prophet Mohammed would have been suitably impressed with the contestants if he were alive today. This statement offended the Muslim Northerners, who declared a "fatwa" on the Southern journalist. The resulting riot led to the death of about 200 people.

In their book, *The Global Media: The New Missionaries of Global Capitalism*, Herman and McChesney (1997) referred to the power of transnational media in influencing the basic assumptions and modes of thought of people and in establishing the capitalist development in developing countries. To a large extent, the educated elite in Nigeria depends on BBC, VOA, CNN, and the global satellite systems (DSTV) as the major sources of information. These sources of news affect the political temperature in Nigeria, inflaming passions and sometimes fueling ethnic and religious tensions through mischief or uninformed interpretations of local events. The constant religious riots in the North often followed similar anti-American or anti-Israeli spillover from global events.

The impact of transnational information flows has also had a tremendous effect on civil uprising and identity formations in Nigeria. For instance, during the Nigerian Civil War (1966-70), the international news media was instrumental in inciting violence in the country. In 2001, a CNN reporter, using a rather unscientific poll, had reported that Nigerians yearned for the return of military rule two years into the new democratic experiment. That open incitement could have served as a green light to an ever-restless military, and had the potential to cause a major civil disturbance

The Rise of Religious Fundamentalism

For the greater part of 2001, there were a series of sectarian conflicts between Christians and Muslims in Kaduna, Jos, and Kano over the introduction of the Sharia, the Muslim legal code. These incessant conflicts and killings continued in parts of Plateau state in 2004, and resulted in the introduction of "emergency rule" in the state of Plateau. In 2002, religious riots took place during the Muslim festival of Ramadan in 2002 following the staging of the *Miss World* beauty pageant in Nigeria, an event which the Muslim community claimed was offensive to their sensibilities. Although Nigeria's constitution recognizes a secular state, *Sharia*—the Islamic code—has been introduced in a number of Northern states beginning with Zamfara state in 2000. Some of the sectarian riots have been ascribed to economic envy. The "settler Igbo," who are Christians, own most of the shops, hotels, and bars in the Muslim Northern Nigeria, and have been easy targets of sectarian violence. Global events such as the U.S. invasion of Afghanistan or the war with Iraq have sometimes inflamed religious passions.

Christian proselytizing through televangelism and open-air crusades with a host of foreign and local religious groups, and a responsive Islamic proselytizing, has turned Nigeria into one giant pseudo-religious state without a corresponding decline in corrupt practices. The basis of such religiosity is not only to provide spiritual succor for the economically marginalized, but also to provide a capitalistic opportunity to accumulate wealth or power for the religious proprietors. Nigerian religious fanatics and sectarian groups, complete with global links through satellite and Internet technology with Saudi, Libyan, or Iranian connections, have become more prominent in the North, while Christian missions and prayerhouses dot the Southern landscape. These divisive tendencies featured more prominently during the entry of Nigeria into the Organization of Islamic States (OIC) in 1986 and the recent debate over the introduction of Sharia. The Christian Association of Nigeria (CAN) had been in the arrowhead of struggles against perceived and real threats against Southern interests (e.g., during the "pro-democracy struggle" against the Abacha regime) while the Supreme Council of Islam was suspected to be used by Northern politicians to protect Northern interests during the Sharia debate under a Southern President Obasanjo

Conclusions

This chapter highlights the social and political impact of globalization without going into great detail on the effect of globalization on other aspects of life, such as governance, technology, agriculture, and the environment. Some of the events presented here are the indirect consequences of the increasing marginalization, inequality, poverty, and desperation of

Africans because of the new global economic order. Some of the negative impacts of globalization may be short term as poor countries struggle to re-adjust to the new economic climate. Furthermore, the impact of globalization is twofold, mixing opportunity with risk, and empowerment with vulnerability in complex ways (Tomlinson 1999).

Every society is built on multiple links, with each link having its own history of interconnectedness (Dijkstra et al. 2001; Gibbon 2002). The impact of globalization on these links has the potential to produce three effects. First, it entails a cultural convergence-the so-called *MacDonaldization* effect, which leads to increasing cultural uniformity and a unipolar, cultural imperialism. The second effect is the harmonizing and differentiating effect, which leads to disenchantment, displacement, and alienation, with a potential to accentuate ethnic differences. The third effect is the bricolage effect, which acknowledges that communities are always in a flux, divided, and contested, and that the majority will always be subject to small-scale resistances by the minority (Gibbon 2002). It has been forcefully argued that global "deterritorialization" or "delocalization" is a myth because of the powerful historical nature of the ethnicity and nationality that mitigate against cultural globalism (Tomlinson 1999). Localism itself, as pointed out by Tomlinson, is not pure, bound, or insular, but constantly changing and in flux. Globalization represents an acceleration of the flux of local events.

We have already seen the harmonizing and bricolage effects on the Nigerian polity because of globalization. Game theory suggests that in the absence of lock-ins, spontaneous inter-ethnic cooperation may occur in a non-linear fashion (Arfi 2001). In Nigeria, the evidence is that there may have been a historical "lock-in" of events. The question then remains—how do we meet the challenges of pluralism given the flux that globalization produces? How do we manage social transformation produced as a result of globalization and how does Africa benefit more from the gains of globalization?

The mantra of development in Africa has been quite simple—reduction in corruption, peace and conflict resolution, better governance, investment in human capital, increased food security, infrastructural provision, etc. Such simplistic solutions often fail to take into account the global dimensions of Africa's economic and social problems: debt peonage, uneven agricultural subsidies, lack of access to technologies, uneven global market conditions, and the corruption climate fostered by transnational networks of electronic fraud and crime syndicates.

It has been estimated that a 30 percent reduction in agricultural subsidies by industrial countries would result in an extra $45 billion in earnings in developing countries. Other measures such as the U.S. AGOA (Africa Growth and Opportunity Act) may improve market access to African products. While global economic integration has been a positive force for growth and poverty reduction, the firm-level evidence is that this has been due to mere churning of plants, leading to increasing wealth for the rich and the demise of the less efficient firms and consequent labor losses. Thus, the challenge is to provide a basket of social protection for the losers, and to limit the social consequences of marginalization as a result of globalization.

Some scholars have argued that Nigeria's ethnic plurality and uneven cultural landscape constitute an albatross inhibiting full global market integration, at least in the short term. The federal principle is Nigeria's novel method of elite accommodation in order to prevent or limit the ethnic dimensions of cultural pluralism. Entrenched in section 14 (Asobie 2001) of the Nigeria Constitution, it seeks to distribute political posts, public office, military appointments, and all forms of political patronage along ethnic lines. This has now been extended to an unwritten understanding among political parties, where there is a call for power-sharing through a rotational formula among Nigeria's geographical zones and a deliberate choice of the top hierarchy of political parties along a mix of religious and ethnic pluralistic lines into a rotational presidency. Although federalism has been widely accepted in Nigeria, there are occasional demands against this "cake-sharing psychosis" that call for a more merit-based system that recognizes Nigeria's secularity and provides for a more rational distribution of political power (Suberu 2001).

One of the more positive political effects of globalization is the convergence of world opinion on issues such as human rights, gender rights, foregiveness, money laundering, and governance. Nigeria and many African countries were subjected to new norms of international behavior, which had a salutary effect on the military. Nigeria had to operate under the political and economic conditionality principle of the G7, which subjected the regimes to sanctions through calls for good governance, and the setting of policies and practices against corruption. The global protest following the sentencing of Nigeria's Amina Lawal to stoning for adultery under the Sharia penal code, is one such example of a desirable global policing. Although such sanctions had an impact on smaller African economies, the impact on Nigerian leaders was quite limited. The New Partnership for Africa (NEPAD) through its peer review mechanism also represents a regional effort to ensure good governance in Africa.

* * *

Acknowledgements

The author wishes to acknowledge the assistance of Professor Adigun Agbaje of the Department of Political Science, University of Ibadan, Nigeria, who provided the author with valuable materials on the subject. I also wish to thank Mrs. Donnet Crooks and Dr. Willie Clarke-Okah for critical review of this manuscript.

References

Aaron, K. K. 2001. Playing without Kits: Towards a Beneficial Participation of Africa in a Globalised World. *Annals of the Social Science Academy of Nigeria* 13: 19-25.

Achebe, C. 1987 *Anthills of the Savannah.* 1987. London: Heinemann.

Anderson, B. 1983. *Imagined Communities: Reflections on the Origin and Spread of Nationalism.* London: Verso.

Arfi, B. "Spontaneous Interethnic Order: The Emergence of Collective Path-Dependent Co-operation." *International Studies Quarterly* 44 (4) (2001): 533-562.

Asobie, A. H. "Globalization: A View from the South." *Annals of the Social Science Academy of Nigeria* 13 (2001): 36-56.

Banjura, Y. 1989. "Crisis and Adjustment: The Experience of Nigerian Workers," in Bade Onimode, ed., *The IMF, World Bank and the African Debt.* London: Zed Press.

Castles, P. "Studying Social Transformation." *International Political Science Review* 22 (1) (2001): 55-84.

Davidson B. 1992. *The Black Man's Burden: Africa and the Curse of the Nation State* New York: Three Rivers Press.

Dijkstra Steven, Geuijen Karin, and Ruijter, Arie. "Multiculturalism and Social Integration in Europe." *International Political Science Review* 22 (1) (2001): 13-32.

Diamond, L. 2002. "Nigeria's Federal Democracy: Will It Survive?" USIP seminar paper.

Gibbon Peter. "Present Day Capitalism, the International Trade Regime & Africa." *Review of Political Economy* 91 (2002): 95-112.

Goff, P. "Invisible Borders: Economic Liberalisation and National Identity." *International Studies Quarterly* 44 (4) (2001): 533-562.

Herman, E., and McChesney, R. 1997. *The Global Media: The New Missionaries of Corporate Capitalism.* London: Cassell.

International Institute for Democracy and Electoral Assistance IDEA. 2002. "Democracy in Nigeria." *Capacity Building* series No. 10.

Joseph, R., Taylor, S., Agbaje, A. 1996. "Nigeria," in M. Kaselus, J. Krieger, and W Joseph, eds., *Comparative Politics at the Crossroad*, 613-689. Lexington, MA: Lexington Press.

Kent, G. 1999. "Globalization and Food Security in Africa," in A. Ogunrinade, R. Onian'go, and J. May, eds., *Not by Bread Alone Food Security and Governance in Africa*, 17-33. Johannesburg: Witwatersrand Press.

Mamdani, M. 1998. "When Does a Settler Become a Native? Reflections on the Colonial Roots of Citizenship in Equatorial and South Africa." *University of Cape Town* New series 208.

Salih, A. E. 2000. "African and Globalization," in *Africa in the Post Cold War Era*, 49-58. Khartoum: International University of Africa Press.

Suberu R. T. 2001 *Federalism and Ethnic Conflict in Nigeria.* Washington, DC: United States Institute for Peace Press

Thornton, J. 1998. *Africa and Africans in the Making of the Atlantic World, 1400-1800.* London: Cambridge University Press.

Tomlinson, J. 1999. *Globalization and Culture.* Cambridge: Polity Press.

Umoren, R. 2001. *Economic Reforms and Nigeria's Political Crisis.* Ibadan: Spectrum Books.

Globalization and Religion on the Web

by Fred W. Riggs

Fred W. Riggs is professor emeritus in the Department of Political Science at the University of Hawai'i at Mānoa.

Religious communities have spread around the world during past millennia, but the speed and extent of their movements have accelerated in recent decades. The World Wide Web is both a force for globalization and a resource available to religious communities. They not only utilize it for their own purposes, but its availability and global reach induces them to modify their messages and practices to make them more widely relevant.

Most communities of faith now have their own sites but they use them for different purposes: some to *promote* adherence to their beliefs and attract new converts; some to encourage inter-faith *cooperation*; and some to promote global peace, environmental sustainability, and *reconciliation*. This paper deals, in turn, with each of these three dispositions. To make some sense out of the wide range of options offered by the new global communications technology, these three themes seem appropriate:

1. *Promotion*: New religious communities, deeply committed to their own beliefs, use the Web to propagate their ideas, win converts, and fight non-believers.
2. *Cooperation*: Established religious communities often use the Internet to reach other communities and encourage them to work together.
3. *Reconciliation*: Some communities committed to peace, nonviolence, en-

vironmentalism, and other such causes use the Web to promote these goals.

The accelerated migration of peoples and the speeding of communications, especially by means of the Internet, have led to the expansion and dispersal of *new religious movements* (NRM). Many of them seek new converts and are confrontational or reactive, insisting on their monopoly of truth, promising the only road to salvation. Their views and posture are examined in section one of this paper, dealing with *Promotion*.

By contrast, long-established *churches* are more willing to compromise and work together—their ecumenical and inter-faith movements are examined in the second section below, under the heading of *Cooperation*.

Not all NRMs are reactive. Some are *adaptive* in the sense that they seek peace and reconciliation on earth and promote environmental sustainability as values consistent with their faith. They are more interested in the mundane consequences of their beliefs than with their supernatural grounds and epistemology. They will be considered in the third section of this paper, on *Reconciliation*.

Each theme will be analyzed by reference to selected websites in which their goals are proclaimed. A wealth of information is now available on the Web about the existence and global extent of innumerable communities of faith.[1] No effort is made here to summarize this data. Rather, by selective references, the perspectives identified above will be illustrated with a few explanatory comments.

Promotion

Although many NRMs are historically recent, some actually have existed for a long time. They are "new" in the sense that they stand apart from established churches, though for different reasons. Some protest compromises accepted by their churches, and others proclaim new doctrines. It is useful to distinguish between these two major causes. The former are called sects and the latter cults. Technically speaking—ordinary usage is not consistent—we may define sects as, *deviant religious organizations with traditional beliefs; and cults, as deviant religious organizations with novel beliefs and practices.*

In general, both sects and cults believe in the ultimate truth of their own faiths based on revelations from the other world. This leads them to resist compromise and use the Internet mainly to promote their beliefs. They typically claim a monopoly on truth as revealed to them by supernatural voices—the term *fundamentalist* is often used to characterize them. Initially used only for some Protestant denominations, the term now has a more generic connotation. We may think of them, generically, as *reactive* communities, founded on strong commitments to resist the compromises often accepted by established churches, or to proclaim new beliefs in contrast with those that have traditionally been accepted.

The Internet now offers reactive (fundamentalist) communities a new vehicle to disseminate their beliefs globally. Their earnestness and persuasive powers generate enthusiastic followers and fierce controversies, sometimes leading to violence. As globalization accelerates, all modern media are used, and especially the Internet, to propagate their beliefs around the world.[2]

When sects and cults are referred to as "new religious movements," we may falsely infer that they are chronologically recent, and no doubt, many are. However, there are quite a few ancient religious movements outside the mainstream of the churches.[3] With such examples in mind, one can see that it is very difficult to simplify the analysis of religious communities.

A useful supplementary distinction cuts across all the categories mentioned above: it is reflected in the suffixes: -*ism* and -*ist*. The former, -ism, appears in the capitalized names of many organized communities: Catholicism, Protestantism, Buddhism, Confucianism, Islamism, Theism, Polytheism, Pantheism, Atheism, etc. By contrast, the ideological or religious orientation of individuals is marked by words ending with -ist: examples are theist, polytheist, pantheist, atheist, Buddhist, Confucianist, and monotheist. This distinction is often important when trying to characterize websites, some of which are sponsored by organized communities (the isms) but, increasingly, many are posted by individuals (the ists). The distinction is often blurred: ardent believers who post sites to propagate their faiths may or may not be embraced by the organized groups they nominally represent.

A couple of examples are illustrative—no effort can be made here to cover the vast literature of this field. A well-known Protestant evangelist is Jerry Falwell who writes:

> Without a doubt the most important message of all times is the Gospel of Jesus Christ. There is no other name on Earth, beneath the Earth or in the Heavens above by which a person can be saved except through the name of Jesus.[4]

Falwell combines fundamentalist evangelism with entrepreneurship and conservative politics, and he operates on a global scale. Other examples can easily be found—there is not enough space to add them here.

A similarly didactic statement of Islamic faith reads:

If anyone desires a religion other than Islam (Submission to Allah), Never will it be accepted of him; and in the Hereafter he will be in the ranks of those who have lost (their selves in the hell fire). *(Qur'an 3:85)*

The only true religion calls for faith in Allah, not any of his creations: "False religion invites man to the worship of creation by calling the creation or some aspect of it God."[5]

The number of such declarations on both Christian and Muslim sites is bewildering and troubling. They claim exclusive truths and paths to salvation, and condemn nonbelievers. The Internet gives them a global arena through which to both advocate and benefit from their convictions. Their home sites, as illustrated above, may be in the United States or anywhere else in the world. Truth, in their view, is found only in revelations from divine sources, not in secular science or empirical proofs.

Information about many such groups and the individual proponents of their religious convictions is readily available in sites for Comparative Religion[6] and the Sociology of Religion.[7] My own Theo-Logic List also contains a segment for Comparative Religion sites.[8] Only a tiny tip of this iceberg can be noted here, but the linked websites open a vast world of relevant perspectives.

Cooperation

Over the centuries, established *churches* have learned to live with the status quo and often compromise in order to survive. Now they find the Internet can help them not only to reach their own members but also to make contact with colleagues in other communities in order to work together. In some countries, an established church enjoys state protection and government subsidies, a relationship that necessarily leads to compromises as politics and economic interests may require. Moreover, when different churches encounter each other— now a ubiquitous phenomenon in the face of globalization and the widespread availability of the Internet—they often reach out to establish inter-faith communication and harmony. Thus, the inherent dynamism that helps churches to survive may also lead them to cooperate with each other.

A familiar and strong ecumenical movement links many Christian denominations. Its main organized expression can be found in the World Council of Churches. According to its website,

The WCC brings together more than 340 churches, denominations and church fellowships in over 100 countries and territories throughout the world, representing some 400 million Christians and including most of the world's Orthodox churches, scores of denominations from such historic traditions of the Protestant Reformation as Anglican, Baptist, Lutheran, Methodist and Reformed, as well as many united and independent churches. While the bulk of the WCC's founding churches were European and North American, today most are in Africa, Asia, the Caribbean, Latin America, the Middle East, and the Pacific.[9]

Liberal Christian theologians have also found ways to reconcile modern science with their religious faith. Some Hindu gurus go even further. They argue that the most advanced discoveries of quantum physics and relativity theory only confirm what the Vedanta and other ancient writings have long known. Here is an example written by Swami Ranganathananda, *Vedanta as the Synthesis of Science and Religion*:[10]

If "man, the known," constituted of his body and its environing world, is the subject of study of the natural sciences, "man, the unknown" is the subject of study of the science of religion. The synthesis of both these sciences is the high function of philosophy as understood in India.... Vedanta has spared us not only the fruitless opposition of reason to faith and vice versa, but also the more dangerous manifestation of this opposition in the form of intolerance, persecution, and suppression of opinion.

The Hindu view of life is tolerant of differences and, unlike Christianity and Islam, makes no effort to proselytize. However, Hindus remain assured that others will see the light and join them. The following text by Swami Vivekananda expresses this view: "The Hindus, like the Jews, do not convert others; still gradually, other races are coming within Hinduism and adopting the manners and customs of the Hindus and falling into line with them."[11] So far, this perspective is not well institutionalized, though it is well expressed by persuasive individuals and groups.

Quasi-Religious Movements

A philosophical orientation that focuses on links between traditional religious norms and secular democratic values is called *Humanism*. The International Humanist and Ethical Union offers this foundational statement:

Humanism is a democratic and ethical life stance, which affirms that human beings have the right and responsibility to give meaning and shape to their own lives. It stands for the building of a more humane society through an ethic based on human and other natural values in the spirit of reason and free inquiry through human capabilities. It is not theistic, and it does not accept supernatural views of reality.[12]

It may be inappropriate to label humanism as a religious movement because it explicitly rejects faith in any supernatural forces or realities, but it expresses a quasi-religious orientation. It relies on reason and empirical evidence rather than faith to maintain an ethical stance that supports democratic and secular idealism as widely understood around the world. It avoids debate about supernatural forces—its members are typically agnostic.

Similarly, *atheists* claim they are not religious because religions are defined by faith in the supernatural.[13] Nevertheless, there are atheist organizations that mimic religious groups in their structure and practices, starting from the premise that there is no God. Although not a "denomination" there is an explicit philosophical position called Positive Atheism.[14] Whether or not atheists actually believe there is no God, they normally profess a strong commitment to the ethical values endorsed by established churches.

Interfaith Movements

Increasingly, in the context of globalization, leaders of different religious communities now reach out to their counterparts in other communities to seek common ground. Although they may not attract widespread popular followings, their perspective seems to be gaining ground.[15] They demonstrate the growing power of movements not only to overcome tensions between different religious communities, but also mobilize them for shared concerns like peace and environmental conservation.[16]

Notable among these movements is the Interfaith Alliance in the United States.[17] According to its website, this organization brings together the spiritual leaders of many different communities. Its main page contains this statement of intent and membership:

On Capitol Hill, through community and online activism, and by focusing media coverage, we work to safeguard religious liberty, ensure civil rights, restore good government, strengthen the public education system, eradicate poverty, and champion a safe and clean environment. With over 150,000 members drawn from more than 65 faith traditions—and those with none at all—and local Alliances in 38 states, The Interfaith Alliance aims to encourage compassion, civility, and mutual respect for human dignity in an increasingly diverse society.

Although the majority of the sixty-five communities represented in this alliance are Christian—Protestant, Catholic, and Orthodox—the list also includes Animists, Baha'i, Buddhists, Mormons, Hindus, Jains, Jews, Muslims, Scientologists, Shintoists, Sikhs, Taoists, Theosophists, Wiccans and Zoroastrians. Explicitly excluded are the intolerant or reactivist communities who insist on their exclusive path to salvation and condemn non-believers. They write:

We actively challenge those, such as the Religious Right, who foster intolerance and degrade the value of a multi-faith nation, instead protecting religious integrity in America by affirming the duty of people of faith and good will to pro-

mote the healing and positive role of religion in public life.[18]

Through a linked Foundation, the Alliance takes stands on many current legislative and other public policy issues. For example, it opposes legislation to support "faith-based" activities, as explained here: "The Interfaith Alliance remains strongly opposed to "faith-based" legislative proposals. Chief among our concerns is the potential impact of charitable choice on the vitality of the prophetic voice of faith, the integrity of religious autonomy, excessive government entanglement in the affairs of religious institutions and the overarching temptation to abuse religion and manipulate faith to achieve political power."[19]

A parallel organization is the World Congress of Faiths, an organization built by individual members of many religious communities. It takes its beginnings from the World's Parliament of Religions, held in Chicago in 1893. A second root was the Religions of Empire Conference, held in London in 1924. Its origins are British as explained thus:

British society has been transformed in the sixty-five years during which the World Congress of Faiths has been in existence. In 1936, London was the centre of an Empire, which included people of many races and religions. Some thirty years later, Britain itself was starting to become multi-ethnic and multi-faith.[20]

Although the basic goal of the World Council of Churches is to foster ecumenical cooperation among different Christian communities (see note 9) it has also sponsored inter-faith dialogue with non-Christians. Its report on *Ecumenical*

Considerations for Dialogue and Relations with People of other Religions, produced in 2002, focuses on the need for dialogue and mutuality, as expressed thus:

> Dialogue must be a process of mutual empowerment, not a negotiation between parties who have conflicting interests and claims. Rather than being bound by the constraints of power relations, partners in dialogue should be empowered to join in a common pursuit of justice, peace and constructive action for the good of all people.[21]

Three types of dialogue are encouraged by the WCC: multilateral, academic, and spiritual. In the first, common issues are addressed such as family, education, and the state; in the second, the focus is on the theological and philosophical bases of their traditions; and in the third, reciprocal participation in the prayer and spiritual life of participating communities. A coalition of different religious groups—Frontier Internship in Mission—has been formed to send young people to work in places where tensions between rival confessions prevails—notably in Iraq, East Timor, Beirut, Amman, Ramallah, and Casablanca.[22] Thus, although starting from an ecumenical Christian foundation, the WCC finds itself seeking reconciliation with many different faiths and using the Web as a medium to support these efforts.

Reconciliation

Faiths that espouse inter-faith understanding, pacifism, and nonviolence, or promote environmental survival also use the Internet to support these causes rather than to proselytize. An instructive example is the Baha'i community, which stresses the important contributions of faith by all major religions. It therefore constitutes a kind of inter-faith faith. A basic premise of this community is that "Each of the great religions brought by the Messengers of God—Moses, Krishna, Buddha, Zoroaster, Jesus, Muhammad—represents a successive stage in the spiritual development of civilization."[23] A letter sent in May/June 2002 by the Baha'i "Universal House of Justice" to religious leaders around the world warned that "danger grows that the rising fires of religious prejudice will ignite a worldwide conflagration the consequences of which are unthinkable." The letter continued, "Tragically, organized religion, whose very reason for being entails service to the cause of brotherhood and peace, behaves all too frequently as one of the most formidable obstacles in the path." In response, according to this report, "Many leaders—whether Buddhist, Christian, Hindu, Jewish, Islamic or other—expressed hope that the message will spur religious leaders and their followers to action."[24]

Although Gandhi-ism is not seen as a religion, it may be viewed as a powerful spiritual force resting on *ahimsa* foundations. This is the Hindu ethic of nonviolence, the importance of not harming people or the environment, of living with gentleness.[25] Although rooted in religious beliefs of different traditions, the basic concept has been adopted by secular movements as well. Mahatma Gandhi said: "Nonviolence is the greatest force at the disposal of mankind. It is mightier than the mightiest weapon of destruction devised by the ingenuity of man." Belief in the power of nonviolence takes many forms in different religious communities. It has also attracted secular political movements, though in many cases the spiritual/secular divide is not apparent.

One of the oldest and most respected religious communities committed to *ahimsa* is the Society of Friends (Quakers). They sponsor Friends for a Non-Violent World.[26] At their site one can find explicit information about how to use the Internet to organize nationally and internationally, for example, in the struggle against the U.S. war in Iraq. An opening paragraph on this site proclaims:

> Nationally, internet-driven, lobbying-oriented organizations like MoveOn.org and direct-action-oriented organizations like International ANSWER innovated new means of immediate, country-wide coordination of actions and campaigns, drawing in and drawing together hundreds of thousands of concerned citizens scattered across the country.

Among the historic pacifist churches, the Mennonites are also noteworthy. Their efforts for peace spurred by the war in Iraq were reported, on March 16, 2003, as follows:

> More than 1,100 people around the globe are fasting for peace between the United States and Iraq, including those who've joined MCC Canada women's fast for peace.[27]

Pax Christi is an international Catholic organization that promotes dialogue among protagonists in conflict situations and encourages inter-faith dialogue. It seeks "opportunities for leaders of religious communities, especially in conflict areas, to listen and learn from one another so together they can help their different faith communities to find a way toward reconciliation."[28]

The Muslim Peace Fellowship encourages cooperation with Christians.[29] A global guide to Muslim communities, available through Islam City, encourages cooperation with non-Muslims.[30] Many communities included in this list have their own inter-faith projects. For example, the Institute of Arabic and Islamic Studies reports: "A historical and unprecedented event took place at the Crystal Cathedral, Garden Grove, California on September 10, 2000. For the first time two preeminent leaders of Islam and Christianity met to share the common ground of their two faiths, which represent more than one half the world population." The leaders were Shaykh Salah Kuftaro and Dr. Robert Schuller.[31]

An internationally active and widely linked inter-faith organization is the Fellowship of Reconciliation. It is currently circulating via the Internet a petition that reads:

> Rather than bringing peace and security to the Iraqi people, the U.S. occupation has brought violence, torture, destruction and chaos. The occupation should be ended...[32]

Not surprisingly, many neo-pagan communities have arisen in recent years and make extensive use of the Web to promulgate their faiths, which are environmentally conscious and often promote environmental sustainability. An example is the Church of All Worlds whose declared mission is "to evolve a network of information, mythology and experience that provides a...stimulus for re-awakening Gaia, and reuniting her children through tribal community dedicated to responsible stewardship and evolving consciousness."[33] A globally scattered network of nests and branches are identified on this site—their members organize closed covens or open groves, and may have a traditional focus or a more eclectic one, concentrate on Druidism, faery magick, ceremonial magick, or ecological activism. Thus, the most ancient beliefs and modern concerns are merging.

Conclusion

In a world that seems to be following a downward spiral into growing violence and terroristic conflict, voices for reason, peace, and reconciliation can be found increasingly on the Internet. Although new religious movements often call for exclusive adherence to a single creed or revelation, we also find global efforts to promote harmony through ecumenical and interfaith movements sponsored by well-established churches. Important faith-based initiatives also promote peace and environmental survival. In sum, religious movements not only take advantage of the Web to promulgate their faith but, increasingly, in response to globalization, they adapt their beliefs to global challenges and post their positions on the Internet. Through the Web, religion and globalization are converging.

Notes

1. A statistical presentation of data about the major religions of the world is available at: http://www.adherents.com/Religions_By_Adherents.html. See also my list of sites for religious information: http://webdata.soc.hawaii.edu/fredr/theo.htm.
2. Definitions and a perceptive analysis of new religious movements can be found in Jeffrey Hadden's *Concepts of our Inquiry*: http://religiousmovements.lib.virginia.edu/lectures/concepts.html. Some examples are offered in Riggs, Faith on the Web, at: http://webdata.soc.hawaii.edu/fredr/FAITH.htm.
3. An interesting example is the Zoroastrian community, which antedates the established churches. They believe that their truly ancient faith hinges on ancestry: only the descendants of Zoroastrians can belong to their community. Since they are now globally dispersed, they have difficulty finding marriage partners. For them, the Internet provides a technological island of security. Among the services the Internet now offers them is a global dating service. Apparently the project is a success as revealed by this remark: *"Since the act of marriage to a fellow Zoroastrian is enjoined in our religion, the Zoroastrian Matrimonial page has been started in an effort to enable far-flung Zoroastrians to contact prospective husbands or wives from among their own religion."* http://www.zoroastrianism.com/. Another influential ancient but very private community is that of the freemasons—see: http://web.mit.edu/dryfoo/www/Masons/index.html.
4. See:http://www.jerryfalwell.com/?a=shelp. On this site one can find a host of related "conservative Christian" institutes, foundations, and seminaries endorsed by Falwell, plus his own autobiography and writings. Among his various enterprises, he is chancellor of Liberty University and writes that since it *"opened in 1971, we now have over 70,000 alumni, 2,500 who are serving as senior pastors in America and an additional 1,000 families who are serving as missionaries of the Gospel across the globe. They studied the Bible right here at Liberty University with some of the greatest Christian professors and Bible scholars in the world!"* I've not found any general list for reactive religious communities, but this list of Apologetics Organizations links many Fundamentalist Protestant groups: http://www.str.org/links/apolorgs.htm.
5. The quotation from the Koran is taken from Islam World: http://www.islamworld.net. This site is by the Al-Huda School, which operates in Washington, DC: http://www.alhuda.org/alhuda/index.html. The following quotation shows the extent of Islamic schools in this area: *"In the Baltimore-Washington DC metro area, there were only 2-3 Islamic schools 5 years ago; this number will soon surpass 10 by the end of this year. If we add to this, the fact that there are nearly a half million Muslims in the Baltimore-Washington DC metropolitan area, and well over 50,000 school age Muslim children, then it be-*

comes very clear that even if we started another 20 schools we could not take care of all our children." The quotation is from a linked American website offering this explanation: "*There are so many sects, cults, religions, philosophies, and movements in the world, all of which claim to be the right way or the only true path to Allah. How can one determine which one is correct or if, in fact, all are correct? False religions all have in common one basic concept with regards to Allah. They either claim that all men are gods or that specific men were Allah or that nature is Allah or that Allah is a figment of man's imagination. Thus, it may be stated that the basic message of false religion is that Allah may be worshipped in the form of His creation. False religion invites man to the worship of creation by calling the creation or some aspect of it God. For example, prophet Jesus invited his followers to worship Allah but those who claim to be his followers today call people to worship Jesus, claiming that he was Allah!*" See The True Religion, by Abu Ameenah Bilal Philipst: http://www.usc.edu/dept/MSA/introduction/truereligion.html.

6. For the bibliography of Comparative Religion, see: http://religion.rutgers.edu/vri/comp_rel.html

7. The Religious Research Association, with a home page at: http://rra.hartsem.edu/Default.htm, promotes sociological research. Their site provides links to a wide range of other organized groups for the comparative study of religions—see http://rra.hartsem.edu/colleagues.htm. Documentation on the major religions (churches) can be found at: http://www.cnn.com/EVENTS/world_of_faith/links.html, and for sects and cults, see: http://hirr.hartsem.edu/org/faith_new_religious_movements.html.

8. Go to http://webdata.soc.hawaii.edu/fredr/THEO.htm.

9. The modern ecumenical movement seeks to promote Christian unity. The WCC site is at: http://www.wcc-coe.org/wcc/who/index-e.html. Its membership list—http://www.wcc-coe.org/wcc/who/mch-e.html—includes a wide range of Protes-

tant denominations and Orthodox churches, but not yet Roman Catholics.

10. See: www.hinduism.co.zanewpage1.htm#Vedanta%20as%20the%20synthesis%20of%20Science%20and% 20Religion. Further evidence of this perspective can be found in Vedanta as the Synthesis of Science and Religion, by Swami Ranganathananda. Quoting Frank Capra's (6/4/2004) Tao of Physics, he writes: "*The basic oneness of the universe is not only the central characteristic of the mystical experience, but is also one of the most important revelations of modern physics. It becomes apparent at the atomic level, and manifests itself more and more as one penetrates deeper into matter, down into the realm of sub-atomic particles. The unity of all things and events will be a recurring theme...of modern physics and the Eastern philosophy.*" http://www.hinduism.co.za/newpage1.htm#Modern%20Physics%20and%20Philosophical%20Reason.

11. For this text and more, see: http://www.hinduism.co.za/newpage15.htm#Conversion.

12. This statement can be found at: http://www.iheu.org/minimum_statement.html. The IHEU was founded in 1952—it holds congresses in different countries. The latest was in Amsterdam, July 2002, where "*humanists from all around the world have 'gathered to celebrate the birth fifty years ago of the International Humanist and Ethical Union (IHEU). During the congress 'The Voice of the World Humanist Congress,' an Internet Webcasting Station has been active transmitting the main events and making its own reportages on the spot.'* Details are given at: http://213.132.199.164/whc/WHC_Online_media.asp."

13. This fine point of belief is discussed at: http://www.abarnett.demon.co.uk/atheism/atheismreligion.html. Barnett writes: "*Atheism Is Not a Religion or a Faith! Atheism, by definition, is the absence of theism. If you cannot say 'I believe in a Deity/God/ Supreme Being' then you are an atheist. If you are not a theist, then you are an atheist...there is a subtle but important difference between 'believing there is no God,' and 'not believing there*

is a God.' The first is a belief, the second is a lack of that belief." Although this claim rejects the idea that atheists share any faith, this website encourages non-believers to sign on and you can find some of their stories at: http://www.abarnett. demon.co.uk/atheism/why_become.html. Moreover, they are organized, as reported at the Atheist Alliance: http:// www.atheistalliance.org.

14. For details, see: http://www.positive atheism.org. Another atheist site worth viewing is called the Secular Web: http:/ /www.infidels.org/index.shtml. Also called "Naturalism," this group believes in the nonexistence of all supernatural beings. They sometimes cluster believers and any such beings as "deistist," but this term seems more properly to belong to a specific set of beliefs which we link with the name of Thomas Jefferson and other founders of the American Revolution. See http://www.deism.com/. They claim that a deist believes... *"in the existence of a God or supreme being but denies revealed religion, basing his belief on the light of nature and reason."* This puts them into opposition with Christians and Muslims whose beliefs stem from a prophet or messiah.

15. See the "Inter-faith" sites at: http:// webdata.soc.hawaii.edu/fredr/ theo.htm#interfaith

16. An overview of the inter-faith movement is offered by Tony Judge in, *Learnings for the Future of Inter-Faith Dialogue*: see: http://laetusinpraesens.org/docs/ diaparl.php.

17. View its site at: http://www.interfaith alliance.org/About/AboutMain.cfm. *"We work to promote interfaith cooperation around shared religious values to strengthen the public's commitment to the American values of civic participation, freedom of religion, diversity, and civility in public discourse and to encourage the active involvement of people of faith in the nation's political life."*

18. www.interfaithalliance.org/ ReligiousResources/ ReligiousResourcesMain.cfm#50.

19. For details, see: http://www.interfaith alliance.org/Issues/IssuesList.cfm?c=51.

20. For more details, see: http:// www.worldfaiths.org/moreinfo.htm.

21. http://www.wcc-coe.org/wcc/what/inter-religious/glines-e.html.

22. Information about this activity can be found at: http://tfim.org. Like the Interfaith Alliance, the WCC welcomes liberal communities but does not accept fundamentalist (reactivist) communities as members. They list their members at: http://www.wcc-coe.org/wcc/links/ church.html. However, they also list unaffiliated congregations at: http:// www.wcc-coe.org/wcc/links/ evanmiss.html but do not explain why they remain outside the membership.

23. Their main site is The Baha'i World, at: www.bahai.org.

24. http://www.onecountry.org/e141/ e14101as_UHJ_Letter.htm.

25. For a definition of ahimsa, see: http:// en.wikipedia.org/wiki/Ahimsa. *Ahimsa is an Eastern spiritual concept of active nonviolence or noninjury, thus kindness and love towards all. It is a central tenet (perhaps the first tenet) of Jainism and yoga. It was introduced to the West by Mahatma Gandhi; the Western civil rights movements, inspired by his actions, engaged in nonviolent protests, led by such people as Martin Luther King Jr."* Gandhi's influence is widespread, as now cultivated by the Gandhi Institute for Nonviolence: http://www.gandhi institute.org. A list of some nonviolent sites is posted at: http:// webdata.soc.hawaii.edu/fredr/ theo.htm#ahi.

26. For details, see: http://www.fnvw.org. The best known and one of the most pro-active Quaker organizations is the American Friends Service Committee, with a site at: http://www.afsc.org.

27. See:news.mennonite.net/complete_press_ release.php3?FORM_id=1387.

28. This quotation is taken from: http:// www.paxchristi.net.

29. See its site at: http://www.mpfweb.org. The Muslim Peace Fellowship supports a site that explains the historical and theological basis for its position. See: http:// www.mpfweb.org/200110_peaces pirit.html. A paragraph in this text reads:

"After his arrival at Medina, the Prophet gave a charter that granted security of life, property, and religion to both Muslims and non-Muslims. He was the first and foremost person who brought a permanent peace between all the conflicting religions of the world.... He asked the people to put faith in all the great religious personalities of the world. He brought unity among the various warring tribes of Arabia."

30. Find the Islam City home site at: http:// islamcity.org.

31. http://www.islamic-study.org. Similar positions can be found in parallel sites for Buddhist, Jewish, Orthodox, Protestant, and other religious communities. Glenn Paige through the Center for Global Nonviolence has published books dealing with Islamic and Buddhist nonviolent teaching and practices, as reported in international conferences. Go to: http:// www.globalnonviolence.org/index2.htm.

32. The FOR site is at: http://www.forusa.org.

33. http://www.caw.org/index.html. Neo-pagans endorse: *"ecological and environmental concerns as well as demonstrating our LOVE for Mother Earth. Our overall purpose is to relink humanity with itself and Nature. Therefore knowledge of the world of Nature and the forces of Nature, are important in this tradition."* Taken from the Welsh Wiccan site: http:// www.tylwythteg.com/public.html. There are many other organized neo-pagan, pantheistic, and indigenous as well as paranormal, new age, and mystic communities, all of which seem to share deep ecological and environmental concerns—see: http://webdata.soc.hawaii.edu/fredr/ theo.htm#pag.

CALL FOR PROPOSALS TO
Toda Institute for Global Peace and Policy Research
RESEARCH PROGRAM, SECOND DECADE, 2006-2016
Human Development, Regional Conflicts, and Global Governance (HUGG2)

In the course of its first decade (1996-2006), the Toda Institute took up three major research programs. HUGG1 (1996-1999) focused on problems of Human Security and Global Governance. GRAD (2000-2003) concentrated on problems of globalization, regionalization, and democratization. The PEACE project (2004-2006) dealt with the problems of peace education, art, culture, and environment. The fruits of this collaboration among over 1000 peace scholars from all five continents have been as follows: over 20 international conferences, 16 volumes, and nine years of publication of *Peace & Policy*, the Institute journal.

During its second decade (2006-2016), the Toda Institute focuses on three major and interlocking global problems, namely Human Development, Regional Conflicts, and Global Governance (HUGG2). The three themes cover global peace and policy problems from micro, meso, and macro perspectives. The post-Cold War genocides in former Yugoslavia, Rwanda, Sudan, the Persian Gulf, Israel-Palestine, and global terrorism suggest that human dignity, security, and development are closely tied to problems of regional conflict and global governance. There seems to be a cultural and institutional lag between development of weapons of mass destruction and global governance. While hit-kill ratios have advanced, the human family has not yet developed a sufficient sense of global responsibility to support and expand the institutions of regional conflict management and global governance. Prolonged periods of perceived or real repression have often created high levels of hatred unleashed in the form of genocides.

During its second decade, the Toda Institute's research program will support the United Nations Development Program's pioneering work on human development. However, it also aims at relating such problems to the issues of conflict management at the regional and global levels. Regional conflicts have been a perennial feature of the world system. The collective security provisions of the UN charter were devised to meet such challenges. However, de facto power plays have often taken precedence over the employment of the collective security measures. As the U.S. invasions of Afghanistan and Iraq have demonstrated, no super-power alone can manage the problems of regional security in conflict-ridden areas. In the interest of world peace and security, the human family needs to devise effective ways and means of handling regional conflicts.

Moreover, the problems of human development and regional conflict cannot be adequately addressed unless the problem of global governance in a post-Westphalian world is seriously addressed. Democratizing global governance is a daunting problem. The UN Charter was drawn at a time that most of the world was destroyed. In addition to the permanent members of the Security Council, other significant stakeholders in global governance have now emerged. The role of the emerging major powers, inter-governmental organizations, global civil society, and transnational financial, industrial, and media corporations call for particular attention. A new global covenant is needed to ensure the survival and prosperity of the human species.

In order to achieve a multicultural dialogue and perspective, each research project will be directed by a Principal Investigator and composed of a team of scholars from different regions of the world. Each proposed project must meet the following conditions:

- A Principal Investigator (PI) that can command the respect and confidence of the project participants.
- Project participants drawn from all parties to the conflict.
- A project proposal, including a plan of study, participants, timeline, budget, and outcome.
- A dialogical method of investigation in which all parties to the conflict have ample opportunity to express their views.
- In a blind review process, approval by the Toda Institute's Research Committee.

Proposal Submission

For the Fiscal Year, April 1, 2006-March 31, 2007, project proposals must be submitted before September 1, 2005. Deadline for subsequent years will be also the first of September of each year. Research proposal must cover the following topics:

Title of the research proposal
Name, title, affiliation, and full address of the Principal Investigator

Name, title, affiliation, and full address of the research team participants,
(N. B.: Participants must come from a variety of countries representing the stakeholders in the problem under investigation.)
Statement of the problem
Review of the literature
Proposed contributions of the research project
Project timetable
Project outcome

Project budget, including the following items: PI honorarium, $1000, participants' honorarium, $500 per person for teams of no more than 12 scholars, project expenses, $1000, air fare and hotel accommodation to the Toda Institute's annual conference for the project participants. Budgets above $25,000 must show other sources of financial support.

Evaluation of the Projects

A Research Committee of prominent peace scholars will be convened to evaluate and select the projects for each fiscal year.

Further Information

For further information, you may write to the Toda Institute for Global Peace and Policy Research, 1600 Kapiolani Blvd., Suite 1111, Honolulu, HI 96814. Tel: 808-955-8231. Fax: 808-955-6476. Email: toda@toda.org.

The Honolulu Conference

The Toda Institute's annual February conference focused on the future of higher education. The conference was held in

Honolulu on February 4-5, 2005. About thirty prominent scholars in the field of higher education attended the conference, including three past and present university presidents. The impact of technological revolution in communications, globalization, and plurality of learning strategies were among the topics covered by the conference. A case study of the problems of governance at the University of Hawai'i raised questions on the future of governance of higher education. The conference participants presented their own visions of higher education in the future. A book of edited papers will be soon published by the Toda Institute to cover the conference topics.

The Madrid Conference

On May 25-27, 2005, the Toda Institute convened its ninth annual conference in Madrid, Spain. The Iberian-American Foundation and the Spanish branch of the Club of Rome co-sponsored the conference. Seven research project teams, including some seventy participants from twenty-nine countries, attended the conference.

Following a plenary, the research teams met in separate workshops to focus on the progress of their own projects. The teams focused on Anti-Racism, Democratization in the Caucasus, Bridging the Global Digital Divide, Peace Journalism, Music for Peace, Islam in Southeast Asia, and Intra-Islamic Dialogue.

A message from Daisaku Ikeda, founder of the Toda Institute, welcomed the participants to the conference. The two plenaries at the beginning and end of the conference were addressed by two distinguished Spanish peace scholars. Ricardo Diex-Hochleitner, honorary president of the Club of Rome, addressed the conference on theme of "Peace Education and Global Citizenship." Federico Mayor Zaragoza, former director-general of UNESCO, spoke to the plenary on "What is a Culture of Peace?"

The conference represented two distinct innovations A team of musicians and musicologists pursued their own project on music for peace while entertaining the conference participants with music from the world. A team of young peace scholars from a variety of countries also attended the conference to pursue their project on bridging the global digital divide.

Conference Group Photo taken in Madrid, Spain.

FORTHCOMING INTERNATIONAL CONFERENCE

Reforming or Transforming the United Nations: Human Development, Regional Conflicts, and Global Governance in a Post-Westphalian World

February 3-5, 2006

To inaugurate its second decade, the Toda Institute is planning an international conference on the United Nations. The conference will take place in California in collaboration with other academic institutions. This prospectus outlines the conference theme.

Since the end of the Cold War, the world has entered a new phase in international relations. Several new actors can be witnessed in an emerging post-Westphalian world. The Westphalian phase (1648-1989) was state-centric. States continue to play a critical role. However, they have been increasingly accompanied by other stakeholders, including Transnational corporations (TNCs), Transnational media corporations (TMCs), intergovernmental organizations (Egos), nongovernmental organizations (NGOs), transnational criminal organizations (TCOs), and transnational terrorist organizations (TTOs). In the meantime, the United Nations has been largely bypassed in the Yugoslav, Rwandan, and Persian Gulf conflicts.

In order to face the daunting challenges of a post-Westphalian world, the proposed international conference aims at going beyond piecemeal UN administrative reforms. It proposes to address the three fundamental issues of global governance facing the twenty-first century. Conceived as micro, meso, and macro challenges, the problems of human development, regional conflict,

and global governance stand at the heart of such challenges. The post-Cold War genocides in former Yugoslavia, Rwanda, and Sudan suggest that human security and human dignity are closely tied together. Prolonged periods of perceived or real repression often create high levels of hatred unleashed in the form of genocides. The international community has not yet devised effective methods for the prevention of such genocides. However, the UN system has significantly contributed to human development through its aid programs and by highlighting the existing problems through the UNDP Human Development Reports.

Regional conflicts have been a perennial feature of the world system. The collective security provisions of the UN charter were devised to meet such challenges. However, de facto power plays have often taken precedence over the employment of the collective security measures. As the U.S. invasions of Afghanistan and Iraq have demonstrated, no super-power alone can manage the problems of regional security. In the interest of world peace and security, The UN needs to devise effective ways and means of handling regional conflicts.

Problems of human dignity and regional conflict cannot be adequately addressed unless the problem of global governance in a post-Westphalian world is seriously addressed. Democratizing global governance is a daunting problem. The UN Charter was drawn at a time that most of the world was destroyed. In addition to the permanent members of the Security Council, other significant stakeholders in global governance have now emerged. A new global covenant is needed to ensure the survival and prosperity of the human species.

The conference will follow a dialogic method. Instead of prepared papers, we request the participants bring with themselves their ideas, experiences, and open minds. We wish to collectively imagine a future world of greater international peace and cooperation. To explore the preconditions for such as world, the conference will explore the following four themes. The themes correspond to the research program of the Toda Institute during its second decade (2006-2016):

1. Reforming or Transforming UN
2. Promoting Human Development
3. Managing Regional Conflicts
4. Democratizing Global Governance.

Participants are asked to bring their vision statements to the conference. Chapters for an edited book will be later assigned to the participants. The resulting volume aims at greater integration of the topic.

Peace Poetry

"Requiem for the Buddhas of Bamiyan"[1]
Karen Kovacik
1st Place in the Nuclear Age Peace Foundation Poetry Contest 2002

If we gain something, it was there from the beginning.
If we lose something, it is hidden nearby.
—Ryokan

Between the empire of China
   and the empire of Rome,
in an oasis along the Silk Road,

you heard pomegranates change hands
   in Latin and Farsi and Greek.
Chinese generals, Persian merchants,

inventors of gunpowder and algebra,
   fanciers of rhubarb and bronze:
all conducted their commerce

in your shadow: you
   who saw monasteries cut from mountains,
you who were sculpted out of sandstone,

who listened to the whispers of Christians;
   who welcomed Muslims and Manicheans,
disciples of Nestor and Zoroaster.

Leopards and lions rolled past you
   in their cages, actors
mimicked peacocks and parrots, travelers

who'd thirsted through the Taklamakan Desert
   gave thanks to plural gods.
You who survived Genghis Khan's cannon,

who saw the British retreat, then Soviets and Americans,
   you whom the Taliban ringed
with burning tires blackening your face,

you with dynamite in your groin, you witness
   to starving farmers, to secret schools for girls:
for fourteen centuries you stood fast

still as Siddhartha
   on the night of his enlightenment,
as much a part of this valley as the wind.

Who will know you now by your absence,
   remembering your before?
When the night comes, who will know you?

When the ash falls, who will know you?
   After earthquakes and eclipses,
whenever there is fire,

how to feel you filling us and leaving us,
   abiding in the grottoes
of our breath?

Note

1.   First place in the Nuclear Age Peace Foundation's Barbara Mandigo Kelly Peace
   Poetry Awards in 2002. Published in *The Poetry of Peace*, edited by David
   Krieger (Santa Barbara: Capra Press, 2003).

PEACE POETRY

Is World War III Upon Us, Or Is This Really Just a Game?

By Genevieve Cora Fraser

Is World War III upon us

Did it start while we were glued

Watching news from the local channel

Nightline, Frontline, CNN or Fox

Did Charlie Rose announce the line-up

Of the predatory pack

Did Larry King look stern, advise us

Or are we lost in history's rush

As the facts speed up and pass us

Did we even stand a chance

Storming Baghdad is behind us

Why retaliate for that

So some bombs are left at Aldgate

King's Crossing to Tavistock Square

Does it mean the war has started

Or did our leaders set the snare

Were they wrestling with woes in Africa

Nestled down in their Glen Eagle lair

Or are we caught in a global shell game

Mind games from Tele to Tube to scare

PEACE POETRY

Can this really be happening to us

Were the warnings really for real

You bomb our cities we'll bomb yours

Now is that fair I ask of you

We're the greatest powers for certain

Ask our public relations crew

When folks doubt

We bombard them

So they haven't got a clue

We're the fakers and deceivers

The world is built on lies

But the money's good

So gee whiz shut your trap

Just visualize

Could Bin Laden be out to teach us

Is Al Qaeda not a game

Though the heads roll

On the nightly news

It's not my head

So I can't complain

Play along we want resources

That fuel our needs and dreams

PEACE POETRY

Our nukes are bigger than their nukes

We'll just scheme and scheme and scheme

Will the euro or the dollar

Or the petro cash win out

Drop another bomb on Iraq

So they haven't got a doubt

Wrapped in flags and god and slogans

We proudly march along

Come join our merry band

Sing our favorite song

We're the biggest and the baddest

But we're nice guys none the less

And we'll squash you like a little bug

If you ever dare protest

You can keep your funny headdress

And plant your silly bombs

We'll raise our warning

To Red Alert

And merrily play along

In Memoriam

Andre Gunder Frank
24 February 1929 to 23 April 2005

Prophet in the Wilderness

Andre Gunder Frank, perhaps the most prolific and controversial Development Economist and Sociologist of the post-war era, best known as the author of "Dependency" theory, died on Saturday in Luxembourg, age 76, after a long battle against cancer. His opus includes some 40 books and nearly a thousand articles and other pieces, in numerous languages, spanning fifty years of global political and economic development. His life and work was full of movement, argument, and counter-argument. Always ahead of his time, his achievement was to repeatedly stand tradition and received theory on their head in field after field (especially Economics, Development Studies, Sociology, and History) and issue after issue. Decades later, many of his ideas have now been generally accepted as events proved his analysis and predictions accurate: the stubborn persistence of Third World poverty and "underdevelopment" despite foreign investment and because of unmanageable debt-servicing imposed by foreign creditors; the failure of "really existing capitalism" in much of the Third World as well as the failure of "really existing socialism" in the former "Second World" (including China) and their re-integration to global capitalism and subsequent partial "Third-Worldization"; the reappearance of persistent structural economic crisis and imbalance in the West (including Japan and the U.S.) and in global capitalism as a whole and the ineffectiveness of Keynesian and fiscal stimulatory means to redress this; the polarizing and fragmenting consequences of "globalization," rendering national states largely incapable of offering real solutions and giving rise to new social movements on global scale that now carry forward the hope for progressive change and at the same time of new rightist, nationalist, ethnic and religious fundamentalist movements that may eventually undermine the democratic culture needed by the former; and finally, a profound rejection of traditional "Eurocentric" theories and understandings of global development and world history in favor of an alternative "humanocentric" world-historical perspective which views the "rise of the West" to global dominance as occurring very "late" and likely to be temporary, and in fact already passing into "history."

He was born Andreas Frank, in Berlin, the son of a pacifist novelist who took him into exile at age four to escape Hitler's Germany. The "Gunder" was added by his high school teammates as a cruel jibe about his slowness on the track field, by comparison with a then famous Swedish runner, Gundar Haag. (As Gunder later explained, "Unfortunately, I did not know how the name was spelled.") His youthful experiences in Hollywood, USA exposed him to his father's circle, which included Thomas Mann and Greta Garbo. He became a Keynesian while studying economics at Swarthmore College, but by the end of his PhD at the University of Chicago (begun in 1950) he had rebelled against his monetarist tutor Milton Friedman and against all Development thinking of U.S. origin, which he saw as "part of the problem" rather than the solution. His rejection of mainstream economics, in favor of an "equity before efficiency" approach focused on the importance of social and political factors, turned him into a maverick who spent the next fifty years energetically and cogently challenging established wisdom and policy on "development" around the world. His early work established the concept of "general productivity" (later known as 'total productivity") and its centrality to measuring "Human Capital and Economic Growth" (1960). It was his 1967 publication of the essay "Sociology of Development and Underdevelopment of Sociology" (rejected by a dozen journals) and his first book "Capitalism and Underdevelopment in Latin America" (also 1967) that catapulted him to international fame, laying the basis for what was to be known as Dependency theory, and its later spin-off, World System theory.

The decisive turning point in his career came when he visited Cuba in 1960 (Che Guevara wrote to Frank asking him for help to transform Cuba's dependent economy) and Ghana and Guinea in Africa. He spent the rest of the 1960s living and working in Latin America, mainly in Brazil, Mexico, and Chile and analyzing their underdevelopment. The Peruvian theorist Anibal Quijano introduced Gunder to his wife of thirty years, Marta Fuentes, a Chilean who shared his passion for social justice and dedication to "change the world." His students at the University of Brasilia included Theotonio Dos Santos and Ruy Mauro Marini, both of whom later became Dependency theorists in their own right. Frank's trenchant analysis of underdevelopment in Brazil, Mexico and Latin America argued directly against not only Keynesian and Monetarist economics and "Modernization" theory, but also against orthodox Marxism

and communist party theory and policy, as well as criticizing the "indigenous" structural reformism of Fernando Henrique Cardoso (once welcomed by Frank at Santiago airport as he fled from the military coup in Brazil in 1964 and later President of Brazil in the 1990s) and Raul Prebisch of CEPAL/ECLA, and the U.S. sponsored "Alliance for Progress." His unrelenting attacks on the inefficacy of existing policies and reformist ideas, and his preference for political revolution (as in Cuba) and socialism earned him a persona non grata status in the U.S. for fifteen years.

He and Marta lived in Santiago, Chile, during the Allende years, where his ideas were coming into favor. Allende, then President of the Senate, met Gunder at the airport to prevent him being instantly deported. Thereafter, their home became a centre of refuge and discussion for intellectuals from across Latin America, until the military coup by General Pinochet on September 11th, 1973 abruptly ended the socialist experiment, democracy, and the lives of countless friends. It was another decisive turning point in Frank's life and career. While Chile became a monetarist "heaven" run by Milton Friedman's "Chicago Boys," Frank became (again) a political exile, this time back to Europe (arriving back in Berlin exactly forty years after fleeing Hitler's regime) and dedicated the next twenty years to analyzing the global crisis and the rampant failures of neo-liberalism and "Reaganomics." It was in this period that he moved beyond Dependency theory, saying that while dependency itself was alive and kicking in the world, its usefulness as a guide to political action had come and gone ("Dependence is Dead! Long Live Dependence and the Class Struggle," 1972). His subsequent work turned increasingly to analysis of the "global crisis of capital accumulation," in both historical and contemporary perspective. His thinking ran parallel to that of others working in the same track, including his long time friend Samir Amin (who he met in Paris during the "events" of 1968), Giovanni Arrighi (who first introduced the "world system" approach to Frank), and Immanuel Wallerstein, who in the 1970s together developed the analysis known as "World-Systems theory."

Frank's copious work on "the crisis" chronicled the disastrous onset of "market ideology" and the return of efficiency before equity in theory and policy. He predicted (in 1974) that the Third World's response to the global crisis would be predicated upon increasing exports to world markets and that this transition to export led growth would be organized under authoritarian regimes (including in East Asia as well as Latin America), while it would inevitably lead to a deeper global depression and the amassing of gigantic unsustainable debts—i.e., to the Debt Crisis and "vastly increased foreign dependence." In the end, Frank felt that "development" itself had "all but disappeared" from discussion, replaced by "only economic or debt crisis management." He continued to analyze the tendencies of globalization, including the replacement of productive investment by financial speculation and the consequent increase in imbalances between regions and countries of the world economic system. He argued that increasing marketization and privatization as responses to the crisis would only further exacerbate underlying poverty, inequality, and marginalization, leading to tremendous pressures on democratic political culture and to the inexorable rise of both new progressive and reactionary social movements to fill the void left by the national state's incapacity and unwillingness to deliver real change.

The final phase of his life and work saw him returning to world development as the main subject of analysis, but this time across all of world history. Working with a co-author (Frank and Gills 1993) he offered an alternative to Eurocentrism which placed the contemporary crisis and globalization in a much longer historical perspective based on the long cycles of world system development going back not only centuries but even millennia. This work led him to conclude, in his final radical rejection of received theories, that we should be brave enough to reject "capitalism" itself as a "scientific" concept, as well as "feudalism" and even "socialism" as separate "modes of production" nor should we any longer look for any real historical "transitions" between them. He argued that "too many big patterns in world history appear to transcend or persist despite all apparent alterations in the mode of production." His final position therefore encapsulated a lifetime of movement and critique, including of his own previous positions. In of his penultimate and perhaps best work, "ReOrient" (1998) and in the unfinished "ReOrient the 19th Century" sequel, he explored the historical method in new directions, again challenging received theory about the "rise of the West" and the supposed role played by the market and "free" trade as opposed to coercion and imperialism. His final analysis of global development included the idea that it is the system as a whole that is the inescapable framework of both analysis and practice and that any "de-linking" from it at "local" or national level is unrealistic, nor will global development ever be "uniform" across the world. He felt that shifts in (temporary) competitive advantage (not always achieved by non-coercive or "market" means alone) and the presence or absence of "hegemonic power" were historically persistent patterns that in a sense define the long term development of the world system. However, he always embodied the idea of both "the pessimism of the intellect" as well as the "optimism of the will" and so left a final admonition—i.e., that the real "global majority," the disadvantaged of the world, should and would act to protect their lives and interests and to improve social existence. He believed to the end that change for the better remains possible.

As a person, Gunder Frank was principled and uncompromising, yet always willing to listen to the evidence and an opposing argument, and even to accept that he was wrong and to change his views. Above all, he was always courageous and never afraid to be unpopular. He gave people the answers they needed not the answers they wanted to hear, even if they did not always want to hear them. He could be difficult at times but his life was always about heart, and he was deeply caring and humane and had many longtime friends.

Within 24 hours of his death, his family received a thousand email and other messages of condolence and support from around the globe. He was above all a generous man, both to his friends and to his critics. He was combative intellectually and thrived upon this approach, but he also possessed a wonderful dry sense of humor, that endeared him to all who knew him well. His attitude to life can perhaps be summed up in his phrase, said to his third and final wife, Alison, "Only two people in this world are always right—the Dalai Lama (who he met and liked, but didn't always agree with) and me," followed by "and only two people in this world know how to load a dishwasher—the Dalai Lama and me!" Gunder Frank is survived by his two sons, Paul and Miguel and three grandchildren. He was still working until two weeks prior to his death in hospital in Luxembourg on Saturday the 23rd of April, 2005.

Barry K. Gills
Newcastle upon Tyne

In Memoriam

Sir Joseph Rotblat
(1908-2005)

A Legacy of Peace

Joseph Rotblat was one of the great men of the 20th century. He was a man of science and peace. Born in Warsaw, Poland in 1908, he was one of those rare individuals who, like Rosa Parks or Nelson Mandela, comes to an intersection with history and courageously forges a new path. In Joseph's case, the intersection with history arrived in 1944 while he was working on the Manhattan Project, the US project to develop an atomic bomb.

Joseph had worked as a scientist toward the creation of an atomic weapon, first in the UK at the University of Liverpool and then at Los Alamos, New Mexico. When he learned in late 1944 that Germany would not succeed in developing an atomic bomb, he believed there was no longer reason to continue work on creating a US bomb. For him, there was only one reason to create an atomic weapon, and that was to deter the German use of such a weapon during World War II. If the Germans would not have an atomic weapon, then there was no reason for the Allies to have one. Joseph was the only scientist to leave the Manhattan Project on moral grounds.

He was the last living signer of the 1955 Russell-Einstein Manifesto, one of the great documents of the 20th century, and he often quoted its final passage: "We appeal, as human beings, to human beings: Remember your humanity and forget the rest. If you can do so, the way lies open for a new paradise; if you cannot, there lies before you the risk of universal death."

He was convinced that countries needed to abolish nuclear weapons and he devoted his life to achieving this goal, as well as the goal of ending war as a human institution. Just prior to his 90th birthday, he said that he still had two great goals in life. "My short-term goal," he said, "is the abolition of nuclear weapons, and my long-term goal is the abolition of war."

Joseph was for many years the General Secretary of the Pugwash Conferences on Science and World Affairs, and later served as president of the Pugwash Conferences. In his work with Pugwash, he was instrumental in bringing together scientists from East and West, so that they could find common ground for ending the Cold War with its mad nuclear arms race. In 1995, Joseph and the Pugwash Conferences were joint recipients of the Nobel Peace Prize.

He began his Nobel acceptance speech by saying, "At this momentous event in my life...I want to speak as a scientist, but also as a human being. From my earliest days I had a passion for science. But science, the exercise of the supreme power of the human intellect, was always linked in my mind with benefit to people. I saw science as being in harmony with humanity. I did not imagine that the second half of my life would be spent on efforts to avert a mortal danger to humanity created by science."

In his speech, he reasoned that a nuclear weapon-free world would be safer than a world with nuclear weapons, but the danger of "ultimate catastrophe" would still exist. He concluded that war must be abolished: "The quest for a war-free world has a basic purpose: survival. But if in the process we learn how to achieve it by love rather than by fear, by kindness rather than compulsion; if in the process we learn to combine the essential with the enjoyable, the expedient with the benevolent, the practical with the beautiful, this will be an extra incentive to embark on this great task."

When Joseph came to Santa Barbara in 1997 to receive the Nuclear Age Peace Foundation's Lifetime Achievement Award for Distinguished Peace Leadership, I asked him, "What gives you hope for the future?" He responded, "My hope is based on logic. Namely, there is no alternative. If we don't do this [eliminate nuclear weapons and engender more responsibility by scientists as well as citizens in general], then we are doomed. The whole existence of humankind is endangered. We are an endangered species now and we have to take steps to prevent the extinguishing of the human species. We owe an allegiance to humanity. Since there is no other way, then we must proceed in this way. Therefore, if we must do it, then there is hope that it will be done."

Earlier this year, JQseph made an appeal to the delegates to the nuclear Non-Proliferation Treaty Review Conference, held in May at the United Nations in New York. "Morality," he wrote, "is at the core of the nuclear issue: are we going to base our world on a culture of peace or on a culture of war? Nuclear weapons are fundamentally immoral: their action is indiscriminate, affecting civilians as well as military, innocents and aggressors alike, killing people alive now and generations as yet unborn. And the consequence of their use could bring the human race to an end." He ended his appeal with his oft-repeated plea, "Remember your humanity."

I visited Joseph at his home in London just a few months ago. He had been slowed down by a stroke and was disturbed that he wasn't able to be as active as he'd been accustomed. But his spirit was strong, and he was still smiling and looking forward. He was as committed as ever to his dual goals of achieving a world without nuclear weapons and without war—goals to which he had devoted the full measure of his energy, intellect and wisdom.

Joseph has left behind a strong legacy of peace. It is our job now to pick up the baton that he carried so well and passionately for so long, and continue his legacy.

David Krieger is president of the Nuclear Age Peace Foundation (www.wagingpeace.org) and the Deputy Chair of the International Network of Engineers and Scientists for Global Responsibility (www.inesglobal.org).

Booknotes

Africa

Kadende-Kaiser, Rose, and Paul Kaiser, eds. 2005. *Phases of Conflict in Africa*. Toronto, Ontario, Canada: De Sitter Publications, 184 pp. $39.95. ISBN: 0-9733978-9-6.

Rittner, Carol, John K. Roth, and Wendy Whitworth, eds. 2004. *Genocide in Rwanda: Complicity of the Churches?* St. Paul, MN: Paragon House, 319 pp. $18.95. ISBN: 1-55778-837-5.

Americas

Callinicos, Alex. 2003. *The New Mandarins of American Power*. Cambridge: Polity Press, 159 pp. $19.95. ISBN: 0-7456-3275-0.

de Ferranti, David, ed. 2003. *Closing the Gap in Education and Technology: World Bank Latin American and Caribbean Studies*. Washington, DC: The World Bank, 216 pp. $25. ISBN: 0-8213-5172-9.

Fink, Arlene. 2004. *Conducting Research Literature Reviews: From the Internet to Paper*. Thousand Oaks, CA: Sage Publications, 243 pp. $37.95. ISBN: 1-4129-0904-X.

Halper, Stefan, and Jonathan Clarke. 2004. *America Alone: The Neo-Conservative and Global Order*. New York: Cambridge University Press, 369 pp. $28. ISBN: 0-521-83834-7.

Halweil, Brian. 2004. *Eat Here: Reclaiming Homegrown Pleasures in a Global Supermarket*. New York: W.W. Norton & Company, 237 pp. $13.95. ISBN: 0-393-32664-0.

Horowitz, Irving Louis. 2004. *Tributes: Personal Reflections on a Century of Social Research*. New Brunswick, NJ: Transaction Publishers, Rutgers, 344 pp. $34.95. ISBN: 0-7658-0218-X.

Kamalipour, Yahya R., and Nancy Snow, eds. 2004. *War, Media, and Propaganda: A Global Perspective*. Lanham, MD: Rowman & Littlefield Publishers, Inc., 261 pp. $75. ISBN: 0-7425-3562-2.

Keever, Beverly Ann Deepe. 2004. *News Zero: The New York Times and The Bomb*. Monroe, ME: Common Courage Press, 374 pp. $19.95. ISBN: 1-56751-282-8.

Martin, Judith N., and Thomas K. Nakayama. 2005. *Experiencing Intercultural Communication: An Introduction*. Columbus, OH: McGraw Hill Higher Education, 315 pp. $61.75. ISBN: 0-07-286289-0.

Moghaddam, Fathali, and Anthony Marsella, eds. 2004. *Understanding Terrorism: Psychosocial Roots, Consequences, and Interventions*. Washington, DC: American Psychological Association, 343 pp. $49.95. ISBN: 1-59147-032-3.

Northcott, Michael. 2004. *An Angel Directs the Storm: Apocalyptic Religion & American Empire*. New York: I.B. Tauris and Co. Ltd, 200 pp. $35. ISBN: 1-85043-478-6.

Ocampo, José , and Juan Martin, eds. 2003. *Globalization and Development: A Latin American and Caribbean Perspective*. Palo Alto, CA: Stanford University Press, 214 pp. $25. ISBN: 0-8047-4956-6.

Oropeza, Lorena. 2005. *¡Raza Si! Guerra No! : Chicano Protest and Patriotism during the Viet Nam War Era*. Berkeley and Los Angeles: University of California Press, 278 pp. $21.95. ISBN: 0-520-24195-9.

Quandt, William B. 2005. *Peace Process: American Diplomacy and the Arab-Israeli Conflict Since 1967*. Washington, DC: Brookings Institution Press, 535 pp. $24.95. ISBN: 0-520-24631-4.

Asia (including the Middle East)

Afaqi, Sabir, ed. 2004. *Tahirih in History: Perspectives on Qurratu'l-'Ayn from East and West*. Los Angeles, CA: Kalimát Press, 292 pp. $29.95. ISBN: 1-890688-35-5.

Association for the Study of Persianate Societies, The. 2003. *Studies on Persianate Societies: 2003*, Vol.1. Stony Brook: State University of New York, 318 pp.

Baker, Osman, and Cheng Gek Nai, eds. 1997. *Islam and Confucianism: A Civilizational Dialogue*. Kuala Lumpur: University of Malaya Press, 233 pp. ISBN: 983-100-016-1.

Bar-Tal, Daniel, and Yona Teichman. 2005. *Stereotypes and Prejudice in Conflict: Representations of Arabs in Israeli Jewish Society*. New York: Cambridge University Press, 483 pp. $85. ISBN: 0-521-80797-2.

Behdad, Ali. 1994. *Belated Travelers: Orientalism in the Age of Colonial Dissolution*. Durham, NC: Duke University Press, 165 pp. $19.95. ISBN: 0-8223-1471-1.

Dahlman, Carl J., and Jean-Eric Aubert. 2001. *China and the Knowledge Economy: Seizing the 21st Century*. Washington, DC: The World Bank, 170 pp. $25. ISBN: 0-8213-5005-6.

Darwish, Mahmoud. 2000. *The Adam of Two Edens: Poems*. Syracuse, NY: Syracuse University Press, 206 pp. $19.95. ISBN: 0-8156-0710-5.

Emirates Center for Strategic Studies and Research, The. 2004. *Annual Book 2004: The Emirates Center for Strategic Studies and Research*. Abu Dhabi, United Arab Emirates: The Emirates Center for Strategic Studies and Research, 245 pp. ISBN: 9948-00-637-2.

Frye, Richard N. 2005. *Greater Iran: A 20th-Century Odyssey*. Costa Mesa, CA: Mazda Publishers, Inc., 368 pp. $45. ISBN: 1-568-59177-2.

Gladney, Dru C. 2004. *Dislocating China: Muslims, Minorities, and Other Subaltern Subjects*. Chicago: The University of Chicago Press, 414 pp. $25. ISBN: 0-226-29775-6.

Glassé, Cyril. 2002. *The New Encyclopedia of Islam: Revised Edition of the Concise Encyclopedia of Islam*. Walnut Creek, CA: AltaMira Press, 534 pp. $46.95. ISBN: 0-7591-0190-6.

Guan, Lee, ed. 2004. *Civil Society in Southeast Asia*. Pasir Panjang: Singapore, 276 pp. $25.9. ISBN: 981-230-257-3.

Khalaf, Samir. 2004. *Civil and Uncivil Violence in Lebanon: A History of the Internationalization of Communal Conflict*. New York: Columbia University Press, 368 pp. $18.5. ISBN: 0-231-12477-5.

Marsh, Ian, Jean Blondel, and Takashi Inoguchi, eds. 1999. *Democracy, Governance, and Economic Performance: East and Southeast Asia*. Tokyo, Japan: United Nations University Press, 371 pp. $24.95. ISBN: 92-808-1039-1.

Menashri, David. 2001. *Post-Revolutionary Politics in Iran: Religion, Society and Power*. London: Frank Cass Publishers, 356 pp. $43.95. ISBN: 0-7146-8121-0.

Milton-Edwards, Beverley. 2004. *Islam and Politics in the Contemporary World*. Malden, MA: Polity Press, 240 pp. $24.95. ISBN: 0-7456-2712-9.

Saikal, Amin, and Albrecht Schnabel, eds. 2003. *Democratization in the Middle East: Experiences, Struggles, Challenges*. Tokyo, Japan: United Nations University Press, 211 pp. $21.95. ISBN: 92-808-1085-5.

Sakr, Naomi, ed. 2004. *Women and Media in the Middle East: Power Through Self-Expression*. New York: I.B. Tauris & Co Ltd, 249 pp. $27.5. ISBN: 1-85043-485-9.

Winslow, Deborah, and Michael D. Woost, eds. 2004. *Economy, Culture, and Civil War in Sri Lanka*. Bloomington: Indiana University Press, 242 pp. $22.95. ISBN: 0-253-21691-5.

Europe (including Eastern Europe)

Elster, Jon. 2004. *Closing the Books: Transitional Justice in Historical Perspective*. New York: Cambridge University Press, 298 pp. $70. ISBN: 0-521-83969-6.

Fernandez-Armesto, Felipe. 1987. *Before Columbus: Exploration and Colonization from the Mediterranean to the Atlantic, 1229-1492*. Philadelphia: University of Pennsylvania Press, 283 pp. $19.95. ISBN: 0-8122-1412-9.

Todorov, Tzvetan, and Bellos David (Trans.). 2003. *Hope and Memory: Lessons from the Twentieth Century*. Princeton, NJ: Princeton University Press, 337 pp. $29.95. ISBN: 0-691-09658-9.

International Relations

Assadourian, Erik, Lori Brown, Alesander Carius, et al. 2005. *State of the World,* *2005: Redefining Global Security*. New York: W. W. Norton & Company, 237 pp. $18.95. ISBN: 0-393-32666-7.

Barnett, Michael, and Martha Finnemore. 2004. *Rules for the World: International Organizations in Global Politics*. Ithaca, NY: Cornell University Press, Sage House, 226 pp. $17.95. ISBN: 0-8014-8823-0.

Bomann-Larsen, Lene, and Oddny Wiggen, eds. 2004. *Responsibility in World Business: Managing Harmful Side-effects of Corporate Activity*. Tokyo; New York: United Nations University Press, 288 pp. $32. ISBN: 92-808-1103-7.

Brown, Amy Benson, and Karen M. Poremski, eds. 2005. *Roads to Reconciliation: Conflict and Dialogue in the Twenty-First Century*. Armonk, NY: M.E. Sharpe, 279 pp. $39.95. ISBN: 0-7656-1333-6.

Christian, David. 2004. *Maps of Time: An Introduction to Big History*. Berkeley: University of California Press, 642 pp. $34.95. ISBN: 0-520-23500-2.

Coicaud, Jean-Marc, and Veijo Heiskanen, eds. 2001. *The Legitimacy of International Organizations*. Tokyo, Japan: United Nations University Press, 578 pp. $39.95. ISBN: 92-808-1053-7.

Collins, Randall. 1998. *The Sociology of Philosophies: A Global Theory of Intellectual Change*. Cambridge, MA: Harvard University Press, 1098 pp. $27.5. ISBN: 0-674-00187-7.

Connelly, Mark, and David Welch, eds. 2005. *War and the Media: Reporting and Propaganda, 1900-2003*. London: I.B. Tauris & Co Ltd, 304 pp. $59.5. ISBN: 1-86064-959-9.

BOOKNOTES

Cooper, Andrew, John English, and Ramesh Thakur, eds. 2002. *Enhancing Global Governance: Towards a New Diplomacy?* Tokyo, Japan: United Nations University Press, 308 pp. $31.95. ISBN: 92-808-1074-X.

Dasgupta, Partha, and Ismail Serageldin, eds. 2000. *Social Capital: A Multifaceted Perspective.* Washington, DC: The World Bank, 424 pp. $25. ISBN: 0-8213-5004-8.

Department for Disarmament Affairs. 2004. *The United Nations Disarmament Yearbook: 2003,* Vol. 28. New York: United Nations, 516 pp. $60. ISBN: 92-1-142250-7.

Goh, Evelyn. 2005. *Constructing the U.S. Rapprochement with China, 1961-1974: From "Red Menace" to "Tacit Ally."* New York: Cambridge University Press, 299 pp. $75. ISBN: 0-521-83986-6.

Gould, Carol C. 2004. *Globalizing Democracy and Human Rights.* New York: Cambridge University Press, 276 pp. $70. ISBN: 0-521-83354-X.

Grunberg, Isabelle, and Sarbuland Khan, eds. 2000. *Globalization: The United Nations Development Dialogue—Finance, Trade, Poverty, Peace-building.* New York: United Nations, 233 pp. $16.95. ISBN: 92-808-1051-0.

Halperin, Morton, Joseph Siegle, and Michael Weinstein. 2005. *The Democracy Advantage: How Democracies Promote Prosperity and Peace.* New York: Routledge, 290 pp. $27.5. ISBN: 0-415-95052-X.

Halweil, Brian, Lisa Mastny, Erik Assadourian, et al.; Linda Starke, ed. 2004. *State of the World 2004.* New York: W. W. Norton & Company, 245 pp. $16.95. ISBN: 0-393-32539-3.

Hardt, Michael, and Antonio Negri. 2004. *Multitude: War and Democracy in the Age of Empire.* New York: The Penguin Press, 427 pp. $27.95. ISBN: 1-59420-024-6.

Held, David. 2004. *Global Covenant: The Social Democratic Alternative to the Washington Consensus.* Malden, MA: Polity Press, 201 pp. $19.95. ISBN: 0-7456-3353-6.

Jolly, Richard, Louis Emmerij, Dharam Ghai, and Frédéric Lapeyre. 2004. *UN Contributions to Development Thinking and Practice.* Bloomington: Indiana University Press, 387 pp. $29.95. ISBN: 0-253-21684-2.

Keating, Tom, and W. Andy Knight, eds. 2004. *Building Sustainable Peace.* Tokyo, Japan: United Nations University Press, 439 pp. $30. ISBN: 92-808-1101-0.

Lo, Fu-Chen, and Yue-Man Yeung, eds. 1998. *Globalization and the World of Large Cities.* Tokyo, Japan: United Nations University Press, 530 pp. $34.95. ISBN: 92-808-0999-7.

Mann, Michael. 2005. *The Dark Side of Democracy: Explaining Ethnic Cleansing.* Cambridge: Cambridge University Press, 580 pp. $24.99. ISBN: 0-521-53854-8.

Marten, Kimberly. 2004. *Enforcing the Peace: Learning from the Imperial Past.* New York: Columbia University Press, 201 pp. $27.95. ISBN: 0-231-12913-0.

Migdal, Joel S., ed. 2004. *Boundaries and Belonging: States and Societies in the Struggle to Shape Identities and Local Practices.* New York: Cambridge University Press, 363 pp. $80. ISBN: 0-521-83566-6.

Miyazaki, Nobuyuki, Zafar Adeel, and Kouichi Ohwada, eds. 2005. *Mankind and the Oceans*. Tokyo; New York: United Nations University Press, 225 pp. $32. ISBN: 92-808-1057-X.

Newman, Edward, and Roland Rich. 2004. *The UN Role in Promoting Democracy: Between Ideals and Reality*. Tokyo; New York: United Nations University Press, 357 pp. $33. ISBN: 92-808-1104-5.

Norris, Pippa, and Ronald Inglehart. 2004. *Sacred and Secular: Religion and Politics Worldwide*. New York: Cambridge University Press, 329 pp. $24.99. ISBN: 0-521-54872-1.

Paris, Roland. 2004. *At Wars End: Building Peace After Civil Conflict*. New York: Cambridge University Press, 289 pp. $65. ISBN: 0-521-83412-0.

Pevehouse, Jon. 2005. *Democracy from Above: Regional Organizations and Democratization*. New York: Cambridge University Press, 248 pp. $29.99. ISBN: 0-521-60658-6.

Rittberger, Volker. 2001. *Global Governance and the United Nations System*. New York: United Nations, 252 pp. $21.95. ISBN: 92-808-1075-8.

Sampson, Gary, ed. 2001. *The Role of the World Trade Organization in Global Governance*. Tokyo, Japan: United Nations University Press, 298 pp. $24.95. ISBN: 92-808-1055-3.

Schechter, Michael, ed. 2001. *United Nations-Sponsored World Conferences: Focus on Impact and Follow-up*. New York: United Nations, 287 pp. $24.95. ISBN: 92-808-1048-0.

Semati, Mehdi, ed. 2004. *New Frontiers in International Communication Theory*.

Lanham, MD: Rowman & Littlefield Publishers, Inc., 306 pp. $32.95. ISBN: 0-7425-3019-1.

Silverblatt, Art, and Nikolai Zlobin. 2004. *International Communications: A Media Literacy Approach*. Armonk, NY: M.E. Sharpe, 295 pp. $24.95. ISBN: 0-7656-0975-4.

Spariosu, Mihai I. 2004. *Global Intelligence and Human Development: Toward an Ecology of Global Learning*. Cambridge, MA: The MIT Press, 287 pp. $23. ISBN: 0-262-69316-X.

Stokhof, Wim, Paul van der Velde, and Yeo Hwee, eds. 2004. *The Eurasian Space: Far More Than Two Continents*. Pasir Panjang: Singapore, 216 pp. $23.9. ISBN: 981-230-255-7.

Toye, John, and Richard Toye. 2004. *The UN and Global Political Economy: Trade, Finance, and Development*. Bloomington: Indiana University Press, 393 pp. $29.95. ISBN: 0-253-21686-9.

Tungodden, Bertil, Nicholas Stern, and Ivar Kolstad, eds. 2004. *Toward Pro-Poor Policies: Aid, Institutions, and Globalization*. Washington, DC: The World Bank, 355 pp. $22. ISBN: 0-8213-5388-8.

World Bank, The. 2002. *Globalization, Growth, and Poverty: Building an Inclusive World Economy*. Washington, DC: The World Bank, 174 pp. $25. ISBN: 0-8213-5048-X.

Young, Mary, ed. 2002. *From Early Child Development to Human Development*. Washington, DC: The World Bank, 406 pp. $35. ISBN: 0-8213-5050-1.

Global Peace and Policy

Toda Institute Book Series

Series Editor: Majid Tehranian

For more information, please consult the webpage of the Toda Institute at <www.toda.org>. To purchase, please contact the publisher directly: